iced

180 very cool concoctions

iced

180 very cool concoctions

Jane Lawson

Photography by Tim Robinson
Styling by Sarah O'Brien

THUNDER BAY
P · R · E · S · S

San Diego, California

Thunder Bay Press
An imprint of the Advantage Publishers Group
5880 Oberlin Drive, San Diego, CA 92121–4794
www.thunderbaybooks.com

ThunderBay
P · R · E · S · S

All notations of errors or omissions should be addressed to Thunder Bay Press, Editorial Department, at the above address. All other correspondence (author inquiries, permissions) concerning the content of this book should be addressed to Murdoch Books, Pier 8/9, 23 Hickson Road, Millers Point NSW 2000, Australia.

NOTE: Those who might be at risk from the effects of salmonella poisoning (the elderly, pregnant women, young children, and those with a compromised immune system) should consult their physician before trying recipes with raw eggs.

ISBN-13: 978-1-59223-695-4
ISBN-10: 1-59223-695-2
Library of Congress Cataloging-in-Publication Data available upon request.

Printed in China by Midas Printing (Asia) Ltd.
1 2 3 4 5 10 09 08 07 06

Design Manager: Vivien Valk
Project Manager: Emma Hutchinson
Editors: Katri Hilden, Emma Hutchinson
Food Editor: Jane Lawson
Design Concept: Marylouise Brammer
Art Direction: Sarah Odgers
Designer: Annette Fitzgerald
Photographer: Tim Robinson
Stylist: Sarah O'Brien
Recipes by: Lee Currie, Ross Dobson, Katy Holder, Leanne Kitchen, Jane Lawson, Barbara Lowery, Nadine McCristal, Paul McNally, Christine Osmond, Rebecca Truda and the Murdoch Books Test Kitchen
Recipe introductions by: Leanne Kitchen
Production: Adele Troeger

Big thanks to Sunbeam for providing us with the ice cream machines for recipe testing and photography.

The publisher and stylist would also like to thank the following companies for generously lending furniture, fabric and tableware for photography: Arte Flowers Sydney, The Bay Tree, Bisanna for the tiles, Brunswick & Fils, Chee Soon & Fitzgerald, Dinosaur Designs, House of Bamboo, Ici et La, Imagine This, Mao and More, Newtown Old Wares (especially for Betty Boop!!), No Chintz, Papaya, Parterre Garden, Publisher Textiles, Spence & Lyda, South Pacific Fabrics, Sticky for the lollypops and sweets, Swarovski for the crystal butterflies, Waterford, Wedgwood, Wheel and Barrow, and Victoria Spring for the dragonflies.

contents

cool world Mmmm. Ice cream. Velvety, luscious, sweet, and rich . . . who doesn't absolutely adore it? The world may be a diverse place, but it seems wherever you come from and wherever you go,

the icy treat is making its mark. And here they are, recipes for global cooling—classics from across the continents, hits from the hemispheres, scoops from across the seas . . .

iced

Historians quibble over who **invented** ice cream; the chief **contenders** are a very mixed bag and include the Roman Emperor Nero, a Chinese ruler of the Tang Dynasty (a highly suspect theory), and the cook of England's King Charles I. Others **believe** that Catherine de Medici, often credited as being the ultimate source of most half-decent **gastronomic** advancements, introduced ice cream to the French court during the 1530s and that the rest, as they say, is history. Whoever that genius was who first churned sweetened milk over ice until it firmed into a decadent, **lickable**, frozen mass may have **melted** into the obscurity of time but he (or she) is everybody's hero.

Of course ice cream is now a more sophisticated substance than its primitive antecedents, and commercial processing, which first started in Baltimore in 1851, has made ice cream rather ubiquitous, but no less a magical or delicious **treat** as a consequence of this. The iced dessert lineup extends beyond ice cream, too. Think of palate-cleansing, refreshingly light sorbets; tingly terrines, gritty **granitas**;

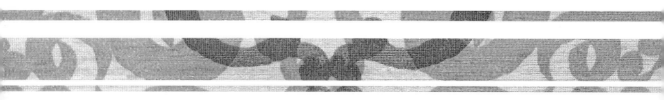

elegant semifreddos; fanciful, layered ice cream cakes; and that most irresistible dinner-party classic, the Baked Alaska.

Icy confections are a global phenomenon, from the gelatos of Italy and the parfaits of France to the deep-fried ice cream of Eastern Asia and that singularly Indian frozen dessert called *kulfi*. Russians love ice cream in the dead of winter, Americans and Australians are known for their impressive per-capita consumption, and in Turkey, they make a curious, stretchy-textured ice cream using an orchid-derived substance called sahlab.

In whatever form they are consumed, and wherever they are enjoyed, it must be conceded that most ice cream eaters are content to purchase ready-made frozen delights; after all, these are widely available, very affordable, and extremely difficult to make at home. Right? Well, yes, except for the difficulty part; iced desserts are, for the most part, simple to whip up. They are made a good deal easier by the use of an ice cream machine, an apparatus that is commonly available, relatively inexpensive, and easy to operate.

Ice creams tend to be egg custard-based. This custard, the legendary **crème anglaise** that professional chefs use to embellish their desserts, is conjured from everyday ingredients (eggs, sugar, cream, milk, and whatever flavorings are required). Sorbets are based upon sugar syrup and, generally, fruit **purées**, although sometimes liqueurs, juices, brewed coffee, and tea are used as well. They are nondairy. A sherbet is made like a sorbet but contains milk as well, walking a **deliciously** fine line between lightly icy and creamily smooth. Fun-to-eat granita, with its coarse-textured crystals, tends to feature direct flavors such as espresso, Campari, or grapefruit, and just requires an occasional stir with a fork to **create** that wonderful, loose texture. A parfait, sometimes called "frozen soufflé," needs no **churning** either, and has a thickened egg-yolk–and–sugar base lightened with whipped cream.

Needless to say, it's well worth the time and effort to make your own icy treats, as the flavor and texture of homemade ice creams, sorbets, parfaits, and the like are **incomparable**.

You can do little in the kitchen that has the same "look what I made" satisfaction than to serve up scoops of your very own ice cream to salivating family and friends, and watch them marvel at the difference from the store-bought flavors they are used to.

If you don't own a machine, good ice cream can still be made. Put the chilled ice cream base into a large metal bowl that allows room for expansion and freeze for about an hour and a half or until the edges start to freeze. Using a wire whisk or electric beaters, set to slow speed and whisk the mixture to break up crystals and aerate the mixture—these two processes are what a machine does mechanically and they are responsible for the soft, scoopable texture of the ice cream. Repeat this procedure at least twice more, freezing the ice cream for an hour and a half between beatings.

Fresh, homemade ice cream will keep for 7–8 days in the freezer (always cover it tightly so it doesn't absorb any other freezer flavors). It is best put in the fridge to soften slightly for 30 minutes before serving. Most of the simpler ice cream recipes in this book will yield around 4 cups of ice cream.

ice cream parlor Way, way back before globalization brought a confusion of choice into our lives and everything seemed so much simpler, the ice cream parlor was a repository of simple

pleasures in the flavors chocolate, strawberry, and vanilla. While the good ol' classics remain hard to beat, leave some space to welcome in some modern classics in the making.

rose geranium sorbet

"I scream, you scream, we all scream for ice cream," so the famous song goes. Once, a screamingly urgent craving for ice cream was satisfied by a trip to the quaint ice cream parlor. Slouching over the long counter and choosing from the array of enticing flavors was just part of the pleasure—the rest involved indulging in an indecently large serving of chilly, soft sweetness eaten in the company of friends. With its atmosphere of innocent, slow-paced fun, the ice cream parlor was partly about ice cream but mostly about simply hanging out. The parlors may be pretty much a thing of the past, but the ethos lives on. There's a time, undoubtedly, for "complex" and "gourmet," but sometimes, all one wants is the honest taste of a good, traditional strawberry or raspberry ice cream, properly made with full-flavored, in-season fruits. Vanilla has become synonymous with "plain"—perhaps because most commercial vanilla ice cream is flavored with fake vanilla extract, which sadly tastes like nothing much at all. But there is nothing everyday about old-fashioned vanilla ice cream, made with proper vanilla beans and perfumed with their diminutive, potent seeds. In fact, many favorite old ice cream parlor themes, with just a bit of tweaking, evolve into creations that might be of the moment, but still retain a comforting, "olde worlde" familiarity. Caramelized pear ice cream, marmalade ice cream, and licorice all-sort ice cream translate into seemingly sophisticated contemporary desserts, but their roots lie firmly in the innocent joys of the ice cream parlor.

vanilla ice cream

1 1/2 cups milk
1 1/2 cups light whipping cream
2 vanilla beans, split lengthwise
  and seeds scraped

2/3 cup superfine sugar
8 large egg yolks

Put the milk, cream, vanilla beans, vanilla seeds, and sugar in a saucepan over medium heat. Stirring, cook for a few minutes or until the sugar dissolves and the milk is just about to boil. Set aside for 15 minutes to infuse. Remove the vanilla beans and gently reheat.

Whisk the egg yolks in a large bowl. Whisk in 1/4 cup of the hot milk mixture until smooth. Whisk in the remaining milk mixture, then return to a clean saucepan and stir constantly over low-medium heat for 8–10 minutes or until the mixture thickens and coats the back of the spoon. Do not allow to boil. Cool slightly, then cover and refrigerate until cold.

Transfer to an ice cream maker and freeze according to manufacturer's instructions. Alternatively, transfer to a shallow metal tray and freeze, whisking every couple of hours until frozen and creamy. Freeze for 5 hours or overnight. Soften in the fridge for 30 minutes before serving.

Makes 4 cups

rum and raisin ice cream

1/2 cup raisins, chopped
2 tablespoons dark rum
3 cups light whipping cream
1 cup milk
3/4 cup superfine sugar

In a small bowl, soak the raisins in the rum. Cover and leave overnight.

Put all the remaining ingredients in a bowl and mix thoroughly.

Transfer to an ice cream maker and freeze according to manufacturer's instructions, adding the raisins halfway through. Alternatively, transfer to a shallow metal tray and freeze, whisking every couple of hours until frozen and creamy, adding the raisins during the final beating. Freeze for 5 hours or overnight. Soften in the fridge for 30 minutes before serving.

Makes 4 cups

For something that starts as burned sugar, caramel adds a sticky allure to oh-so-creamy ice cream.

caramel ice cream

$2/3$ cup superfine sugar
1 cup light whipping cream
6 egg yolks
$2^1/2$ cups milk
1 vanilla bean, split lengthwise and seeds scraped
waffle cones, to serve (optional)

To make the caramel, put half the sugar in a heavy-based saucepan over low–medium heat until it dissolves and starts to caramelize—tip the saucepan from side to side as the sugar cooks to help it color evenly. Remove from the heat and carefully add the cream (it will spatter). Stir over low heat until the caramel melts again.

Whisk the egg yolks and remaining sugar until light and fluffy. Put the milk, vanilla bean, and vanilla seeds in a saucepan and bring just to a boil, then pour into the caramel. Bring back to a boil and pour over the egg yolk mixture, whisking continuously. Remove the vanilla bean.

Pour the custard into a clean saucepan and stir constantly over low–medium heat for 8–10 minutes or until the mixture thickens and coats the back of the spoon. Do not allow the mixture to boil. Set aside to cool slightly, then cover and refrigerate until cold.

Transfer to an ice cream maker and freeze according to manufacturer's instructions. Alternatively, transfer to a shallow metal tray and freeze, whisking every couple of hours until frozen and creamy. Freeze for 5 hours or overnight.

Soften in the fridge for 30 minutes before serving. Serve scooped into waffle cones, if desired.

Makes 4 cups

caramel ice cream

sherry trifle ice cream

1/2 cup instant custard powder	4 tablespoons fresh strawberry
1/2 cup milk	purée
3 egg yolks	1/4 cup confectioners' sugar
2 1/2 cups light whipping cream	6 mini jelly rolls
1/2 cup superfine sugar	4 tablespoons sweet sherry
1 teaspoon vanilla extract	

Blend the custard powder, milk, and egg yolks. Pour into a saucepan with the cream and sugar. Stir over medium heat for 5 minutes or until the mixture boils and thickens. Remove from the heat and stir in the vanilla. Cover with plastic wrap and cool slightly, then refrigerate until cold.

Transfer to an ice cream maker and freeze according to manufacturer's instructions. Alternatively, transfer to a shallow metal tray and freeze, whisking every couple of hours until frozen and creamy.

Put the purée and confectioners' sugar in a saucepan and stir well. Bring to a boil over medium–high heat and cook for 5 minutes to thicken slightly.

Thinly slice the mini jelly rolls and moisten with sherry. Layer the ice cream, mini jelly rolls, and purée in a bar pan, then cover and freeze until firm.

Makes 4 cups

black currant sorbet

2 cups superfine sugar

3 tablespoons light corn syrup

5 cups black currants, stalks removed

2 tablespoons lemon juice

4 tablespoons crème de cassis (black currant liqueur)

Put the sugar and light corn syrup in a saucepan with 1 cup water. Stir over medium heat until the sugar dissolves, then bring to a boil and cook for 2–3 minutes. Remove from the heat and cool completely.

Put the black currants and lemon juice in a blender with half of the cooled syrup and mix to a thick purée. (Alternatively, push the fruit through a sieve to purée, then mix with the lemon juice and syrup.) Add the remaining syrup and crème de cassis and mix well.

Transfer to an ice cream maker and freeze according to manufacturer's instructions. Alternatively, transfer to a shallow metal tray and freeze, whisking every couple of hours until frozen and smooth. Store in the freezer until ready to serve.

Makes 4 cups

Tangy lemon curd, dreamy vanilla ice cream, and a touch of toasted coconut add up to a taste of tongue-tingling bliss.

lemon delicious ice cream

lemon curd
3 egg yolks
1/2 cup superfine sugar
2 teaspoons lemon zest, grated
1/3 cup lemon juice
1/3 cup unsalted butter, chopped

1/2 cup dried coconut
1 quantity vanilla ice cream (see page 16) or 4 cups store-bought

To make the lemon curd, beat the egg yolks and sugar and strain into a heatproof bowl. Add the lemon zest, juice, and butter. Set the bowl over a pan of barely simmering water, making sure the base of the bowl does not touch the water. Stir over low–medium heat for 8–10 minutes or until the mixture thickens and coats the back of a spoon. Do not allow to boil. Cool slightly, cover with plastic wrap, and refrigerate until cold.

Meanwhile, put the coconut in a small frying pan and stir over medium heat for 3 minutes or until lightly golden. Set aside to cool.

Remove the ice cream from the freezer and allow to soften slightly. Pour into a bowl, then add the coconut and $3/4$ cup of the lemon curd and stir well. Return to the freezer and whisk every 30 minutes or so until frozen. Soften in the fridge for 30 minutes before serving.

Serving suggestion: You can spoon the ice cream and lemon curd into ramekins, smooth the surface, top with extra toasted coconut, and freeze until ready to serve. It is also delicious sandwiched between fresh waffles.

Note: If you don't have time to make the lemon curd, use a good-quality version from a gourmet food store or your local farmer's market.

Makes 4 cups

lemon delicious ice cream

chocolate ice cream

1^1/$_2$ cups milk
1^1/$_2$ cups light whipping cream
^{1}/$_2$ cup superfine sugar
5 egg yolks, lightly beaten

1 teaspoon vanilla extract or
   crème de cacao
1^1/$_2$ cups dark chocolate, grated

Put the milk, cream, and sugar in a saucepan over medium heat. Stirring constantly, cook for a few minutes or until the sugar dissolves and the milk is just about to boil. Remove from the heat.

Whisk the egg yolks and vanilla in a large bowl. Whisk in ^{1}/$_4$ cup of the hot milk mixture until smooth. Whisk in the remaining milk mixture, then return to a clean saucepan and stir constantly over low–medium heat for 8–10 minutes or until the mixture thickens and coats the back of a spoon. Do not allow to boil.

Remove from the heat, then stir in the chocolate until melted. Cool slightly, then cover and refrigerate until just chilled. Transfer to an ice cream maker and freeze according to manufacturer's instructions. Alternatively, transfer to a shallow metal tray and freeze, whisking every couple of hours until frozen and creamy. Freeze for 5 hours or overnight. Soften in the fridge for 30 minutes before serving.

Makes 4 cups

strawberry ice cream

1$^1/_2$ cups milk
1$^1/_2$ cups light whipping cream
$^1/_2$ cup superfine sugar
5 egg yolks

1$^2/_3$ cups very ripe strawberries,
  puréed and sieved

Put the milk, cream, and sugar in a saucepan over medium heat. Stirring constantly, cook for a few minutes or until the sugar dissolves and the milk is just about to boil. Remove from the heat.

Whisk the egg yolks in a large bowl. Whisk in $^1/_4$ cup of the hot milk mixture until smooth. Whisk in the remaining milk mixture, then return to a clean saucepan and stir constantly over low–medium heat for 8–10 minutes or until the mixture thickens and coats the back of a spoon. Do not allow the mixture to boil. Set aside to cool slightly, then cover and refrigerate until cold. Stir in the puréed strawberries.

Transfer to an ice cream maker and freeze according to manufacturer's instructions. Alternatively, transfer to a shallow metal tray and freeze, whisking every couple of hours until frozen and smooth. Freeze for 5 hours or overnight. Soften in the fridge for 30 minutes before serving.

Makes 4 cups

multicolored licorice ice cream

coconut meringue
2 egg whites
1/2 cup superfine sugar
1 cup dried coconut
1 tablespoon cornstarch

half quantity of berry ice cream
   (made with raspberries;
   see page 95) or 2 cups
   store-bought

licorice ice cream
1/3 cup soft eating licorice,
   chopped
1 cup milk
3/4 cup light whipping cream
1/4 cup superfine sugar
dash of black food coloring

mango ice cream
2/3 cup milk
1/3 cup superfine sugar
1/2 cup light whipping cream
2/3 cup fresh mango purée

Preheat the oven to 300°F. Cover two cookie sheets with baking paper and draw three 10 x 3-inch rectangles on the baking paper. To make the coconut meringue, beat the egg whites in a small bowl using electric beaters until stiff peaks form. Gradually add the sugar, beating well after each addition, then stir in the combined coconut and cornstarch. Spread evenly over the rectangles. Bake for 15 minutes or until just firm. Turn the oven off and leave to cool in the oven with the door slightly ajar.

Lightly grease a bar pan and line completely with baking paper. Spread the raspberry ice cream evenly into the prepared pan. Top with a coconut meringue and freeze.

To make the licorice ice cream, stir the licorice, milk, and cream together in a small saucepan over low heat until the licorice is soft and melting. Press through a strainer to remove any lumps. Add the sugar, stir until dissolved, then allow to cool. Tint a deeper color with food coloring if desired. Pour into a shallow metal container and freeze until firm. Chop the mixture, beat in a large bowl with electric beaters until thick and creamy, then spread over the meringue and top with another meringue. Freeze.

To make the mango ice cream, put the milk and sugar in a small saucepan and stir over low heat until the sugar dissolves. Remove from the heat, stir in the cream, and set aside to cool. Stir in the mango purée, then pour into a metal container and freeze until semifrozen. Chop the mixture and beat in a large bowl with electric beaters until thick and creamy, then spread over the meringue, top with the remaining meringue, cover, and freeze until firm. When ready to serve, invert the bar pan onto a cutting board, remove the plastic, and cut into slices.

Note: You can freeze all three ice creams at once to save on preparation time. The ice creams can also be made in an ice cream maker.

Serves 6–8

multicolored licorice ice cream

lavender ice cream

10 stems organic lavender, washed and dried	1 small strip lemon zest
	$3/4$ cup superfine sugar
3$1/2$ cups heavy whipping cream	6 egg yolks

Put the lavender, cream, lemon zest, and sugar in a saucepan over medium heat. Stirring constantly, cook for a few minutes or until the sugar dissolves. Remove from the heat and strain through a fine sieve.

Whisk the egg yolks in a large bowl. Gradually whisk in the lavender mixture until smooth, then return to a clean saucepan and stir constantly over low–medium heat for 8–10 minutes or until the mixture thickens and coats the back of a spoon. Do not allow to boil. Pour the mixture into a chilled baking dish and set aside to cool slightly, then cover and refrigerate until cold.

Transfer to an ice cream maker and freeze according to manufacturer's instructions. Alternatively, transfer to a shallow metal tray and freeze, whisking every couple of hours until frozen and creamy. Freeze for 5 hours or overnight. Soften in the fridge for 30 minutes before serving.

Makes 4 cups

34

irish cream ice cream

2 large eggs, separated
3/4 cup superfine sugar
1/3 cup Irish cream liqueur
1 heaped cup mascarpone
   cheese
1 cup whipped heavy cream

Line a 6-cup freezerproof container with plastic wrap. Whisk the egg yolks and 1/4 cup of the sugar in a bowl until pale. Whisk in the liqueur.

Beat the egg whites in a clean dry bowl until stiff peaks form, then gradually beat in the remaining sugar until glossy.

Fold the mascarpone through the egg yolk mixture, then fold in the cream. Gently fold through the egg whites. Pour into the prepared container and freeze for 5 hours or overnight.

To serve, turn out of the container and stand for 5 minutes. Cut into slices.

Serves 6–8

This over-the-top assemblage of fruit, ice cream, nuts, and jelly is a New York native, but is especially popular in Great Britain.

knickerbocker glory

3-ounce packet of raspberry gelatin
1¹/₂ cups frozen raspberries, thawed, juice reserved
¹/₃ cup confectioners' sugar
³/₄ cup heavy whipping cream
15 hazelnuts (optional)
2 peaches, diced
1 large mango, diced
1 quantity vanilla ice cream (see page 16) or 4 cups store-bought
6 glacé cherries

Make the gelatin according to the packet instructions and chill until set.

Meanwhile, put the thawed raspberries and juice in a plastic sieve over a bowl, then push the raspberries through the sieve using a wooden spoon to remove the seeds. Sieve in half the confectioners' sugar and stir to dissolve. Set aside.

Whip the cream with the remaining confectioners' sugar until stiff peaks form. Chill until needed.

Meanwhile, dry-fry the hazelnuts in a frying pan over high heat for 1–2 minutes, tossing the pan regularly. Cool slightly, then rub off the skins and chop roughly.

To assemble, mash the gelatin with a fork to break it up. Divide the raspberry juice and diced fruit among six tall serving glasses. Top with the gelatin and a scoop of ice cream. Finish with a big dollop of whipped cream, a sprinkling of nuts, and a glacé cherry for the top. Serve with long spoons for digging out the delicious bits at the bottom.

Serves 6

knickerbocker glory

black forest ice cream balls

2 cups canned, pitted black cherries
2 1/4 cups almonds, flaked
2 quantities of vanilla ice cream
   (see page 16) or 8 cups
   store-bought

7 ounces dark chocolate
1 1/2 tablespoons Copha (white
   vegetable shortening)

Cover two cookie sheets with foil and put them in the freezer. Drain the cherries and pat dry with paper towels. Toast the almonds on a cookie sheet at 350°F for 5 minutes or until golden. Leave to cool.

Push a cherry into the ice cream. Using an ice cream scoop dipped in cold water, take a scoop of ice cream from around the cherry. Mold into a small ball, roll in toasted almonds, and set on a cookie sheet in the freezer. Continue rolling and freezing until all the cherries are coated.

Melt the chocolate and Copha in a double saucepan (or a heatproof bowl over a pan of gently simmering water) and leave to cool a little.

Using a spoon, quickly dip the ice cream balls in the chocolate and put them on a frozen cookie sheet. Serve as soon as the chocolate sets or freeze until ready to serve.

Serves 10

coffee and hazelnut ice cream

6 egg yolks
2/3 cup superfine sugar
2 cups milk
1 cup light whipping cream

1/3 cup crème de cafe
  (coffee liqueur)
1 cup toasted hazelnuts,
  skinned and chopped

Place the egg yolks and sugar in a heatproof bowl over a saucepan of simmering water, making sure the base of the bowl does not touch the water. Beat until light and fluffy.

In a separate saucepan, gently heat the milk. Pour into the egg yolk mixture and stir constantly over low–medium heat for 8–10 minutes or until the mixture thickens and coats the back of a spoon. Do not allow to boil. Set aside to cool slightly, then stir in the cream, coffee liqueur, and hazelnuts. Cover and refrigerate until cold.

Transfer to an ice cream maker and freeze according to manufacturer's instructions. Alternatively, transfer to a shallow metal tray and freeze, whisking every couple of hours until frozen and creamy. Freeze for 5 hours or overnight. Soften in the fridge for 30 minutes before serving.

Makes 4 cups

Quick, get the kids off to bed so the grown-ups can dig into this whiskey-mellow indulgence. Truly delectable!

chocolate whiskey bar

1²/₃ cups chopped good-quality dark chocolate
¹/₄ cup unsalted butter, softened
4 egg yolks
1¹/₄ cups light whipping cream
2 teaspoons natural vanilla extract
2 tablespoons whiskey
cocoa powder, for dusting
chocolate sauce, dessert wafers, or extra cream, to serve (optional)

Line a bar pan with plastic wrap. Place the chocolate in a heatproof bowl. Bring a small saucepan of water to a simmer, remove from the heat, and put the bowl over the saucepan, being careful not to let the base of the bowl touch the water. Stir the chocolate over the hot water until melted. Alternatively, melt the chocolate in the microwave for 1 minute on High (100%), stirring after 30 seconds. Allow to cool.

Whisk the butter and egg yolks in a small bowl until thick and creamy, then whisk in the cooled chocolate mixture.

In another bowl, whisk the cream and vanilla until soft peaks form. Fold in the whiskey. Using a metal spoon, fold the cream and chocolate mixtures together until just combined.

Pour the mixture into the prepared bar pan, cover with plastic wrap, and freeze for 2–3 hours, overnight, or until firm. Remove from the freezer, remove from the mold, and carefully peel away the plastic wrap. Smooth the wrinkles using a flat-bladed knife, then transfer to a serving plate and dust with cocoa. Cut into slices to serve on its own, or serve with some chocolate sauce, dessert wafers, or extra cream.

Note: This dessert is firm, but will not freeze as hard as ice cream because it contains alcohol. It will keep in the freezer for up to 1 week.

Serves 6

chocolate whiskey bar

marmalade ice cream

1½ cups milk
1½ cups light whipping cream
½ teaspoon orange zest, grated
¼ cup superfine sugar

¼ cup Seville orange
   marmalade
¼ cup sweet marmalade
8 egg yolks

Put the milk, cream, orange zest, and sugar in a saucepan over medium heat. Stirring constantly, cook for a few minutes or until the sugar dissolves and the milk is just about to boil. Remove from the heat.

Whisk the marmalades and egg yolks in a large bowl, then whisk in ¼ cup of the hot milk mixture. Whisk in the remaining milk mixture, then return to a clean saucepan and stir constantly over low–medium heat for 8–10 minutes or until the mixture thickens and coats the back of a spoon. Do not allow to boil. Set aside to cool slightly, then blend in a food processor until smooth. Cover and refrigerate until cold.

Transfer to an ice cream maker and freeze according to manufacturer's instructions. Alternatively, transfer to a shallow metal tray and freeze, whisking every couple of hours until frozen and creamy. Freeze for 5 hours or overnight. Soften in the fridge for 30 minutes before serving.

Makes 4 cups

lemon and lime sherbet

2 cups superfine sugar
1/3 cup lemon juice
1/3 cup lime juice
1 1/2 tablespoons lemon zest,
   grated
1 1/2 tablespoons lime zest,
   grated
4 egg whites

Put the sugar and 2 cups of water in a saucepan and stir over low heat until the sugar dissolves. Stir in the lemon juice, lime juice, lemon zest, and lime zest. Set aside to cool.

Transfer to an ice cream maker and freeze according to manufacturer's instructions. Alternatively, transfer to a shallow metal tray and freeze, whisking every couple of hours until frozen and smooth.

Beat the egg whites until soft peaks form. Fold the egg whites through the sherbet mixture and freeze again until set.

Makes 4 cups

Sour cream always adds a certain "something"—this smart offering will impress the socks off discerning dinner guests.

sour cream ice cream

1¼ cups sour cream
1 cup light whipping cream
1 vanilla bean, split lengthwise
    and seeds scraped
½ cup superfine sugar
5 egg yolks

1 cup canned cherries, drained,
    to serve (optional)
almond tuiles or biscotti, to
    serve (optional)

Put the sour cream, cream, vanilla bean, vanilla seeds, and sugar in a saucepan over medium heat. Stirring constantly, cook for a few minutes or until the sugar dissolves and the milk is just about to boil. Remove from the heat. Remove the vanilla bean.

Whisk the egg yolks in a bowl until well combined. Strain the cream mixture through a sieve into the egg mixture and whisk together well. Return to a clean saucepan and stir constantly over low–medium heat for

8–10 minutes or until the mixture thickens and coats the back of a spoon. Do not allow the mixture to boil. Set aside to cool slightly, then cover and refrigerate until cold.

Transfer to an ice cream maker and freeze according to manufacturer's instructions. Alternatively, transfer to a shallow metal tray and freeze, whisking every couple of hours until the ice cream is frozen and creamy in texture. Freeze for about 5 hours or overnight. Soften in the fridge for 30 minutes before serving.

To serve, scoop the ice cream into bowls, sprinkle with cherries if using, and perhaps accompany with almond tuiles or biscotti.

Makes 4 cups

sour cream ice cream

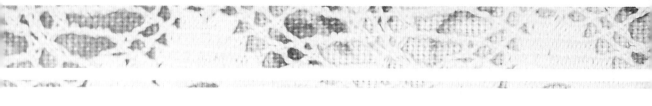

strawberry sorbet

1¹/2 cups superfine sugar
3 cups fresh strawberry purée
strawberries and whipped
    cream, to serve (optional)

Put the sugar and 1 cup of water in a saucepan. Stir over low heat until the sugar dissolves. Remove from the heat and allow to cool.

Stir the strawberry purée into the cooled sugar syrup and pour into a metal tray. Put in the freezer until cold.

Transfer to an ice cream maker and freeze according to manufacturer's instructions. Alternatively, transfer to a shallow metal tray and freeze, whisking every couple of hours until frozen and smooth. Freeze for 5 hours or overnight. Store in the freezer until ready to serve.

Serve with extra strawberries and whipped cream, if desired.

Makes 4 cups

after-dinner mint chocolate balls

2 quantities of vanilla ice cream
(see page 16) or 8 cups store-
bought, slightly softened
four 1¼-ounce chocolate-
peppermint bars

1¼ cups good-quality dark
chocolate, finely chopped

Cover a cookie sheet with foil and put it in the freezer. Put the ice cream in a large bowl. Crumble the chocolate-peppermint bars and mix through. Return the mixture to the ice cream container and freeze until firm.

Scoop the ice cream into large balls. Wearing plastic gloves, mold them into firm balls. Place on the lined cookie sheet and freeze until hard.

Put the chocolate in a heatproof bowl and place over a saucepan of just-simmering water, making sure the base of the bowl does not touch the water. Stir the chocolate until melted, remove from the heat, and stir until completely smooth.

Spoon the chocolate over the ice cream balls and freeze for 1 hour or until the balls are frozen and the chocolate has set.

Serves 8–10

53

This peachy-cream dessert captures the essence of summer—naturally, use the ripest, juiciest peaches money can buy.

peach ice cream

2¹/₂ cups light whipping cream
1¹/₂ cups superfine sugar
8 egg yolks
4 peaches
2 tablespoons lemon juice
¹/₃ cup superfine sugar, extra

Put the cream and sugar in a saucepan over medium heat. Stirring constantly, cook for a few minutes or until the sugar dissolves and the cream is just about to boil. Remove from the heat.

Whisk the egg yolks in a bowl. Gradually whisk in the hot cream mixture until smooth. Return to a clean saucepan and stir constantly over low–medium heat for 8–10 minutes or until the mixture thickens and coats the back of a spoon. Do not allow to boil. Set aside to cool slightly, stirring occasionally.

Peel the peaches and chop them into pieces. Put the flesh in a food processor with lemon juice and extra sugar. Process for 20 seconds or until finely puréed. Stir into the custard.

Transfer to an ice cream maker and freeze according to manufacturer's instructions. Alternatively, transfer to a shallow metal tray and freeze, whisking every couple of hours until frozen and creamy. Freeze for 5 hours or overnight. Soften in the fridge for 30 minutes before serving.

Serving suggestion: Serve garnished with slices of fresh peach—or perhaps drizzled with fresh raspberry purée for a quick peach Melba!

Makes 4 cups

peach ice cream

wheat bread ice cream

1 cup milk
2/3 cup superfine sugar
4 egg yolks
3 cups finely grated fresh wheat
    bread crumbs (do not use dry
    bread crumbs for this recipe)

2 1/2 cups light whipping cream
1 1/2 tablespoons dark rum
orange zest strips, to garnish

Put the milk and sugar in a saucepan over medium heat. Stirring constantly, cook for a few minutes or until the sugar dissolves and the milk is just about to boil. Remove from the heat.

Whisk the egg yolks in a large bowl. Whisk in 1/4 cup of the hot milk mixture until smooth. Whisk in the remaining milk mixture, then return to a clean saucepan and stir constantly over low–medium heat for 8–10 minutes or until the mixture thickens and coats the back of a spoon. Do not allow to boil. Set aside to cool slightly, fold in the bread crumbs, then cover and refrigerate until cold.

Beat the cream until soft peaks form. Stir in the rum. Carefully fold the cream into the cold custard, then pour into a container and freeze for 4 hours or until lightly frozen. Soften in the fridge for 30 minutes before serving. Serve garnished with orange zest strips.

Makes 4 cups

brandy and apple ice

3 large cooking apples,
    peeled and chopped
2 cups apple juice
3 tablespoons lemon juice

$1^1/2$ tablespoons lemon zest,
    finely grated
1 cup superfine sugar
$1/4$ cup brandy

Put the apples in a saucepan with 2 tablespoons of water and cook over medium heat for 10–15 minutes or until soft. Mash until smooth.

Combine the mashed apples, apple juice, lemon juice, lemon zest, sugar, and brandy in a bowl. Allow to cool to room temperature.

Transfer to an ice cream maker and freeze according to manufacturer's instructions. Alternatively, transfer to a shallow metal tray and freeze, whisking every couple of hours until frozen and smooth. Freeze for 5 hours or overnight. Store in the freezer until ready to serve.

Makes 4 cups

59

Parfait means "perfect" in French, which perfectly describes this perfectly lush, perfectly easy dessert.

frozen chocolate parfait

6 egg yolks
1/2 cup superfine sugar
1 1/4 cups good-quality dark chocolate, finely grated
1 1/4 cups good-quality milk chocolate, finely grated
1 vanilla bean, split lengthwise and seeds scraped
1 cup milk
1 1/2 cups light whipping cream
berry sauce, to serve (optional)

Line a greased 5-cup terrine mold with two layers of plastic wrap, allowing the plastic to extend over the sides. Put the egg yolks in a bowl and gradually whisk in the sugar until thick and pale. Place the grated dark and milk chocolate in separate bowls and set aside.

Put the vanilla bean and seeds in a small saucepan with the milk. Slowly bring to a boil, then remove from the heat. Discard the vanilla bean.

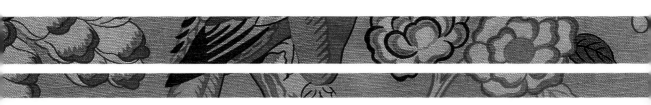

Gently pour the milk onto the egg yolks, whisking constantly. Return the mixture to a clean saucepan and stir constantly over low–medium heat for 8–10 minutes or until the mixture thickens and coats the back of a spoon. Do not allow to boil.

Divide the hot custard between the grated chocolate and mix thoroughly until the chocolate has melted. Allow to cool completely. Beat the cream with electric beaters until soft peaks form. Divide evenly between the cooled chocolate mixtures, and gently fold in. Carefully pour the dark chocolate mixture into the terrine. Freeze for 30 minutes or until firm.

Pour the milk chocolate mixture over the back of a spoon onto the dark chocolate mixture to form an even layer, then smooth the top. Cover with baking paper and freeze overnight or until completely frozen. Just before serving, carefully remove the parfait from the terrine. Slice the parfait and serve with a berry sauce, if desired.

Serves 8

frozen chocolate parfait

raspberry ice cream pots

1 quantity berry ice cream
(made with raspberries;
see page 95) or 4 cups
store-bought
1²/₃ cups raspberries, fresh or
frozen

¹/₃ cup macadamia nuts, toasted
1 tablespoon coconut, toasted
and shredded

Divide half the ice cream among eight ¹/₂-cup ramekins or freezerproof cups and smooth over. Put the raspberries over the top, then the macadamias, and lightly press them down into the ice cream.

Spread the remaining ice cream over the top and smooth over. Freeze for 30 minutes or until firm.

To serve, either dip the bases of the ramekins into warm water and invert onto serving plates, or serve in the ramekins, sprinkled with coconut.

Note: This recipe can be adapted using your favorite seasonal fruits—for example, use mango or peach ice cream and serve with fresh mango or peach slices.

Serves 8

rose geranium sorbet

1¼ cups superfine sugar
9 lemons
6 (8 if small) organic rose
   geranium leaves, crumpled

2 egg whites
rose geranium leaves and
   flowers, to garnish (optional)

Put the sugar in a saucepan with 2½ cups of water. Finely grate the zest of one lemon and add it to the saucepan. Heat over low heat, stirring to dissolve the sugar, then bring to a boil. Add the geranium leaves and allow to boil for 6 minutes. Set aside to cool.

Squeeze the juice from the lemons and strain into the cooled syrup. Mix well, then pour into a cold freezer tray or a metal bowl. Freeze until the mixture just begins to ice over. Empty the mixture into a bowl and discard the geranium leaves. Whisk until smooth but not melted.

Beat the egg whites until stiff but not dry, then fold lightly through the mixture and return to the tray. Cover and freeze for 4 hours or until firm. Store in the freezer until ready to serve. Pile the sorbet into chilled glasses and serve decorated with rose geranium flower and leaves, if desired.

Makes 4 cups

Tart, tangy rhubarb is sweetly matched with masses of sugar and a lingering kiss of vanilla—don't forget the cream!

vanilla-scented rhubarb sorbet

3 pounds (about 12 stems) rhubarb
2 cups superfine sugar
1$\frac{1}{2}$ vanilla beans, split lengthwise and seeds scraped
cream, to serve (optional)

Wash the rhubarb and trim the ends. Chop the stems into $^3/_4$-inch lengths and toss into a saucepan. Add the sugar and 2 cups of water, and stir over low heat until the sugar dissolves. Add the vanilla beans and seeds and mix together well.

Bring to a boil, then reduce the heat to low–medium. Cook partially covered for 5 minutes or until the rhubarb is very soft. Remove from the heat and set aside to cool slightly, then remove the vanilla beans. Transfer to a food processor and purée until smooth.

Transfer to an ice cream maker and freeze according to manufacturer's instructions. Alternatively, transfer to a shallow metal tray and freeze, whisking every couple of hours until frozen and smooth. Freeze for 5 hours or overnight. Store in the freezer until ready to serve.

To serve, break up the crystals with a fork, then spoon the sorbet into eight small serving glasses. Drizzle a little cream over the top if desired, and serve immediately.

Serves 8

vanilla-scented rhubarb sorbet

white chocolate ice cream

3/4 cup superfine sugar
1/2 teaspoon cream of tartar
4 egg whites
2 cups light whipping cream

1 1/4 cup good-quality white
   chocolate, melted

Put the sugar, 1/2 cup of water, and the cream of tartar in a saucepan. Stir over low heat without boiling until the sugar dissolves. Bring to a boil, reduce the heat slightly, then allow to boil without stirring for 15 minutes or until a teaspoon of the syrup mixture dropped into cold water forms a soft ball. Set aside to cool slightly.

Whisk the egg whites in a large bowl until soft peaks form. Gradually add the sugar syrup in a thin stream, beating constantly until thick and glossy.

In a separate bowl, whip the cream until soft peaks form. Fold the whipped cream into the egg white mixture. Add the melted chocolate and mix well. Pour into a 4-cup bar pan and freeze for 5 hours or until firm. Soften in the fridge for 30 minutes before serving.

Makes 4 cups

earl grey granita

2/3 cup superfine sugar
3 Earl Grey tea bags
zest of 1 lemon, cut into strips

Put the sugar and 1 cup of water in a saucepan and stir over low heat for 1–2 minutes or until the sugar dissolves. Bring to a boil and cook for 5–6 minutes or until syrupy.

Bring 4 cups of water to a boil, then transfer to a large bowl. Add the tea bags and lemon zest, then allow to steep for 3 minutes. Discard the tea bags and stir in the sugar syrup. Refrigerate until cool, then remove the lemon zest. Pour into a shallow tray and freeze for 2 1/2 hours or until the mixture starts to freeze around the edges.

Scrape the frozen edges back into the mixture with a fork. Repeat every 30 minutes for about 3 hours or until evenly sized ice crystals form. If you are preparing the granita ahead of time, store it in the freezer and scrape once again just before serving. To serve, scrape into dishes with a fork.

Serves 4–6

Praline—just a fancy name for smashed-up caramel and nuts—
is used here in a mascarpone and white chocolate surprise.

praline ice cream with caramel bark

$2/3$ cup blanched almonds, toasted
$1/2$ cup superfine sugar
$3/4$ cup light whipping cream
1 heaped cup mascarpone cheese
1 cup white chocolate, melted and cooled
2 tablespoons sugar
fresh figs, to serve (optional)

Line a cookie sheet with foil, brush the foil lightly with oil, and sprinkle the almonds on top. Put the superfine sugar in a small saucepan over low heat. Tilt the pan slightly (do not stir) and watch until the sugar melts and turns golden caramel—this should take 3–5 minutes.

Pour the caramel over the almonds and leave until set and cold. Break into chunks, put in a plastic bag, and crush with a rolling pin or process briefly in a food processor until crumbly.

Whip the cream until stiff peaks form. In a large bowl, mix together the mascarpone and melted chocolate. Using a metal spoon, fold in the whipped cream and crushed praline. Transfer to a 4-cup bar pan, cover with baking paper, and freeze for 5 hours or overnight.

To make the caramel bark, line a cookie sheet with foil and brush lightly with oil. Sprinkle the sugar evenly onto the tray and place under a hot broiler for 2 minutes or until the sugar melts and is golden—check frequently toward the end of the cooking time, as the sugar may burn quickly. Remove from the heat and leave until set and completely cold. Then break the caramel into shards. Soften in the fridge for 30 minutes before serving. Serve with the caramel shards and perhaps with some fresh figs.

Makes 4 cups

praline ice cream with caramel bark

rosemary, carrot, and orange granita

1/4 cup superfine sugar
2 small rosemary sprigs,
   leaves picked

3/4 cup fresh carrot juice
1/2 cup orange juice, freshly
   squeezed and strained

Put the sugar, 1/3 cup of water, and the rosemary leaves in a small saucepan and stir over high heat until the sugar dissolves. Bring to a boil, then remove from the heat and allow to cool slightly. Cover and refrigerate overnight to let the flavor develop.

Pour the carrot and orange juices into a bowl. Strain the rosemary syrup and stir 1/3 cup into the juice mixture. Pour into a chilled shallow tray and freeze for 2 1/2 hours or until the mixture starts to freeze around the edges.

Scrape the frozen edges back into the mixture with a fork. Repeat every 30 minutes for 3 hours or until evenly sized ice crystals form. If you are preparing the granita ahead of time, store it in the freezer and scrape once again just before serving. To serve, scrape a small quantity of the granita into dishes with a fork. Enjoy as a refreshing palate cleanser.

Serves 4–6

pistachio ice cream

1/3 cup pistachios, shelled
5 large egg yolks
heaping 1/3 cup superfine sugar
2 cups light whipping cream

1/4 cup shelled pistachios, extra,
chopped

Blanch the pistachios in a saucepan of boiling water for 1 minute. Drain well, then rub off the skins. Grind the pistachios in a spice grinder or with a mortar and pestle until smooth.

Put the egg yolks and sugar in a bowl and beat for 2–3 minutes or until thick and pale. Whisk in the pistachio paste, then the cream. Pour into a saucepan and stir constantly over low–medium heat for 8–10 minutes or until the mixture thickens and coats the back of a spoon. Do not allow to boil. Set aside to cool slightly, then cover and refrigerate until cold.

Transfer to an ice cream maker and freeze according to manufacturer's instructions. Alternatively, transfer to a shallow metal tray and freeze, whisking every couple of hours until frozen and creamy. Freeze for 5 hours or overnight. Soften in the fridge for 30 minutes before serving.

Makes 4 cups

Strange but true: goat cheese, so tangy, citric, and smooth, isn't just great in salads—it makes fabulous savory ice cream, too.

goat cheese ice cream

2$\frac{1}{2}$ cups light whipping cream
1 cup milk
2 tablespoons brown onion, roughly chopped
6 lemon thyme sprigs
1 small garlic clove, peeled and smashed
$\frac{1}{2}$ teaspoon black peppercorns
$\frac{1}{4}$ teaspoon sea salt
4 large egg yolks
1$\frac{1}{3}$ cups crumbled full-flavored goat cheese
2 tablespoons light whipping cream, extra

Put the cream, milk, onion, lemon thyme, garlic, peppercorns, and sea salt in a saucepan over medium heat. Cook for a few minutes, until the mixture is just about to boil. Remove from the heat, then cover and set aside for 15 minutes. Pour the mixture through a sieve into a clean saucepan and gently reheat.

Whisk the egg yolks in a large bowl. Whisk in 1/4 cup of the hot milk mixture until smooth. Whisk in the remaining milk mixture, then return to a clean saucepan and stir constantly over low–medium heat for 8–10 minutes or until the mixture thickens and coats the back of a spoon. Do not allow to boil.

In a small bowl, combine the goat cheese and remaining cream. Whisk the cheese into the cream mixture until the cheese melts. Set aside to cool slightly, then refrigerate until cold.

Transfer to an ice cream maker and freeze according to manufacturer's instructions. Alternatively, transfer to a shallow metal tray and freeze, whisking every couple of hours until frozen and creamy. Freeze for 5 hours or overnight. Soften in the fridge for 30 minutes before serving.

Serving suggestion: This savory ice cream is terrific with plum tomato halves that have been roasted with sugar, thyme, and balsamic vinegar.

Makes 4 cups

goat cheese ice cream

pimm's granita

3/4 cup superfine sugar

3 cups dry ginger ale

2 tablespoons freshly squeezed
   lemon juice, strained

2 tablespoons freshly squeezed
   orange juice, strained

1 cup Pimm's

1 lemon, sliced

6 cucumber strips

6 mint leaves

Put the sugar and 1/2 cup of the ginger ale in a small saucepan and stir over low heat until the sugar dissolves. Reduce the heat and simmer for 3–4 minutes, then set aside to cool.

Stir the remaining ginger ale, lemon juice, orange juice, and Pimm's into the cooled sugar syrup. Pour into a shallow tray and freeze for 2 1/2 hours or until the mixture starts to freeze around the edges.

Scrape the frozen edges back into the mixture with a fork. Repeat every 30 minutes for about 3 hours or until evenly sized ice crystals form. If you are preparing the granita ahead of time, store it in the freezer and scrape once again just before serving in six tall glasses, each garnished with a slice of lemon, a strip of cucumber, and a mint leaf.

Serves 6

apricot and orange blossom sorbet

3/4 cup superfine sugar
1/4 cup light corn syrup
7 ripe apricots, halved and
    pitted

2 tablespoons lemon juice,
    or to taste
1/2 teaspoon orange blossom
    water, or to taste

Combine the sugar, powdered glucose, and 1 1/4 cups of water in a saucepan and stir over low heat until the sugar dissolves. Bring to a boil, add the apricots, and boil gently for 5 minutes. Remove from the heat and set aside until cool.

Purée the apricot mixture in a blender until smooth, then strain through a fine sieve into a bowl. Stir in the lemon juice and orange blossom water and refrigerate until chilled.

83

Transfer the mixture to an ice cream maker and freeze according to manufacturer's instructions. Alternatively, transfer to a shallow metal tray and freeze, whisking every couple of hours until frozen and smooth. Freeze for 5 hours or overnight. Store in the freezer until ready to serve.

Makes 4 cups

Sweets for the sweet—showcasing nature's ambrosial offering, the pear, made even sweeter with condensed milk.

caramelized pear ice cream

7 ounces dried pears
14-fluid ounce can sweetened condensed milk
1 cup light whipping cream
1 cup milk
$2/3$ cup firmly packed soft brown sugar
5 egg yolks
caramel topping, to serve (optional)

Soak the pears overnight in a little water. Put the undrained pears in a small saucepan with the soaking liquid, adding water to just cover if needed. Bring to a simmer, then cover and cook over low heat for 20 minutes or until very soft. Set aside to cool, drain well, chop finely, and refrigerate.

Preheat the oven to 350°F. Put the condensed milk in a small ovenproof saucepan with a tight-fitting lid, then set it in a baking dish. Pour in enough boiling water to come halfway up the side of the dish, then bake for $1^1/2$ hours or until the milk turns deep caramel. Allow to cool slightly.

Combine the condensed milk, cream, milk, and sugar in a saucepan over medium heat. Stirring constantly, cook for a few minutes or until the sugar and condensed milk dissolve and the mixture is just about to boil. Remove from the heat.

Whisk the egg yolks in a large bowl, then whisk in $1/4$ cup of the hot milk mixture until smooth. Whisk in the remaining milk mixture, then return to a clean saucepan and stir constantly over low–medium heat for 8–10 minutes or until the mixture thickens and coats the back of a spoon. Do not allow to boil. Cool slightly, then refrigerate until cold.

Transfer to an ice cream maker and freeze according to manufacturer's instructions, adding the pears just as the ice cream is ready. Alternatively, transfer to a shallow metal tray and freeze, whisking every couple of hours until frozen and creamy, adding the pears during the final beating. Freeze for 5 hours or overnight. Soften in the fridge for 30 minutes and serve with caramel topping if desired.

Makes 4 cups

caramelized pear ice cream

oatmeal and cinnamon ice cream

2¹/₂ cups light whipping cream
1¹/₂ cups milk
¹/₂ cup soft brown sugar
2 cinnamon sticks
1 teaspoon vanilla extract

4 large egg yolks
³/₄ cup rolled oats, lightly
   toasted
maple syrup, to serve (optional)

Put the cream, milk, sugar, cinnamon, and vanilla in a saucepan over medium heat. Stirring constantly, cook for a few minutes or until the sugar dissolves and the mixture is just about to boil. Remove from the heat, cover, and set aside for 15 minutes. Discard the cinnamon sticks and gently reheat.

Whisk the egg yolks in a large bowl. Whisk in ¹/₄ cup of the hot cream mixture until smooth. Whisk in the remaining cream mixture, then return to a clean saucepan and stir constantly over low–medium heat for 2 minutes or until the mixture thickens and coats the back of a spoon. Do not allow to boil. Cool slightly, then refrigerate until cold.

Transfer to an ice cream maker and freeze according to manufacturer's instructions. Alternatively, transfer to a shallow metal tray and freeze, whisking every couple of hours until frozen and creamy. Mix in the oats and freeze overnight. Serve drizzled with maple syrup if desired.

Makes 4 cups

honey and toffee bar ice cream

3 eggs, separated
1/4 cup honey
1 1/4 cups light whipping cream

two 2-ounce thin, chocolate-
coated toffee bars

Whisk the egg yolks in a large bowl until light and fluffy. Add the honey and beat until thick and pale.

Beat the cream until stiff peaks form. In a clean, dry bowl, beat the egg whites until stiff peaks form. Using a metal spoon, fold the cream into the egg whites. Next, fold the cream mixture into the honey mixture.

Chop one of the toffee bars into small pieces and stir through the ice cream. Pour into a 6-cup container and freeze for 5 hours or until firm. Soften in the fridge for 30 minutes before serving.

Just before serving, chop the second toffee bar into pieces and sprinkle over the ice cream.

Makes 4 cups

The cocktail hour meets ice cream hour—a private meeting at once suave, smooth, spicy, and seductively seditious.

brandy alexander ice cream

1 cup milk
2¼ cups light whipping cream
1 cup superfine sugar
8 egg yolks
⅓ cup brandy
2 tablespoons dark crème de cacao (chocolate liqueur)
freshly grated nutmeg or finely grated dark chocolate, to serve

Put the milk, cream, and sugar in a saucepan over medium heat. Stirring constantly, cook for a few minutes or until the sugar dissolves and the milk is just about to boil. Remove from the heat.

Whisk the egg yolks in a large bowl. Whisk in ¼ cup of the hot milk mixture until smooth. Whisk in the remaining milk mixture, then return to a clean saucepan and stir constantly over low–medium heat for 8–10 minutes or until the mixture thickens and coats the back of a spoon.

Do not allow the mixture to boil. Set aside to cool slightly, then refrigerate until cold.

Stir the brandy and crème de cacao into the custard to combine.

Transfer to an ice cream maker and freeze according to manufacturer's instructions. Alternatively, transfer to a shallow metal tray and freeze, whisking every couple of hours until the ice cream is frozen and creamy in texture. Freeze for 5 hours or overnight. Soften in the fridge for 30 minutes before serving.

Serve scoops of the ice cream in cocktail glasses. Sprinkle with grated nutmeg or sprinkle finely grated chocolate over the ice cream.

Makes 4 cups

brandy alexander ice cream

apple and pear sorbet

4 large green apples, peeled,
    cored, and chopped
4 pears, peeled, cored, and
    chopped
1 strip lemon zest

1 cinnamon stick
$1/4$ cup lemon juice
$1/3$ cup superfine sugar
2 tablespoons Calvados or Poire
    William liqueur, optional

Put the apples and pears in a large deep saucepan with the lemon zest, cinnamon stick, and enough water to just cover the fruit. Cover and gently poach over low–medium heat for 6–8 minutes or until tender. Remove the lemon zest and cinnamon stick. Purée the fruit in a food processor with the lemon juice until smooth.

Put the sugar in a saucepan with $1/3$ cup of water, bring to a boil, and simmer for 1 minute. Stir in the fruit purée and liqueur.

Transfer to an ice cream maker and freeze according to manufacturer's instructions. Alternatively, transfer to a shallow metal tray and freeze, whisking every couple of hours until frozen and creamy. Freeze for 5 hours or overnight. Serve in small glasses or bowls.

Makes 4 cups

berry ice cream

1 cup light whipping cream
1 cup milk
1 cup superfine sugar
5 egg yolks

2 cups berries, such as
raspberries or blueberries,
puréed and strained

Put the cream, milk, and sugar in a saucepan over medium heat. Stirring constantly, cook for a few minutes or until the sugar dissolves and the milk is just about to boil. Remove from the heat.

Whisk the egg yolks in a large bowl until well combined, then add the puréed berries. Whisk in ¼ cup of the hot milk mixture until smooth. Whisk in the remaining milk mixture, then return to a clean saucepan and stir constantly over low–medium heat for 8–10 minutes or until the mixture thickens and coats the back of a spoon. Do not allow the mixture to boil. Cool slightly, then cover and refrigerate until cold.

Transfer to an ice cream maker and freeze according to manufacturer's instructions. Alternatively, transfer to a shallow metal tray and freeze, whisking every couple of hours until the ice cream is frozen and creamy in texture. Freeze for about 5 hours or overnight. Soften in the fridge for 30 minutes before serving.

Makes 4 cups

95

Utterly decadent, inexcusably lovely, this exquisite ensemble gives "death by chocolate" a whole new name.

chocolate truffle ice cream

chocolate truffles
1 cup chopped good-quality dark chocolate
1¹/2 tablespoons unsalted butter, softened
1¹/2 tablespoons light whipping cream
1 tablespoon rum or brandy
unsweetened cocoa powder, for dusting

1¹/2 cups milk
1¹/2 cups light whipping cream
3/4 cup superfine sugar
1 vanilla bean, split lengthwise and seeds scraped
6 large egg yolks

To make the chocolate truffles, put the chocolate and butter in a heatproof bowl. Fill a saucepan one third full of water and bring to a simmer. Sit the bowl on top of the saucepan, making sure the bowl does not touch the water. When the mixture has melted, remove from the heat. Stir until smooth.

Put the cream and rum in a small saucepan and bring just to a boil, then stir into the chocolate until glossy. Allow to cool, then refrigerate until firm. Using two teaspoons, take scant half-teaspoons of the mixture and form into irregular capsule shapes. Gently toss in cocoa powder to coat, shaking off any excess. Freeze in a single layer on a lined tray.

Put the milk, cream, sugar, vanilla bean, and vanilla seeds in a saucepan over medium heat. Stirring constantly, cook until the sugar dissolves and the milk is just about to boil. Remove from the heat and discard the vanilla bean.

Whisk the egg yolks in a large bowl. Whisk in $1/4$ cup of the hot milk mixture until smooth. Stir in the remaining milk mixture, then return to a clean saucepan and stir constantly over low–medium heat for 8–10 minutes or until the mixture thickens and coats the back of a spoon. Do not allow to boil. Cool slightly, then refrigerate until cold. Transfer to an ice cream maker and freeze according to manufacturer's instructions, adding the truffles just before the ice cream is ready.

Makes 4 cups

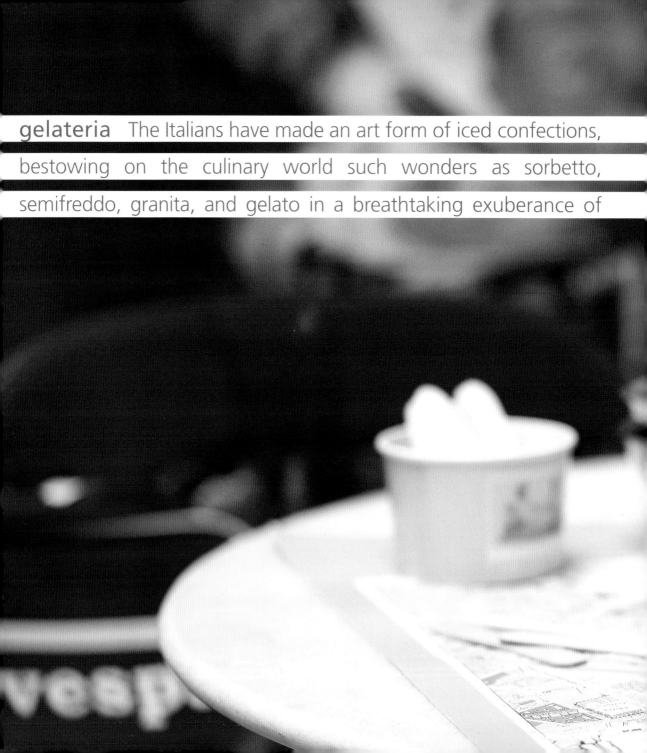

gelateria The Italians have made an art form of iced confections, bestowing on the culinary world such wonders as sorbetto, semifreddo, granita, and gelato in a breathtaking exuberance of flavors. Let a Bellini sorbet sweep you off to Venice, a cantaloupe version take you to a swanky little trattoria in Rome, or a refreshing tomato granita have you dreaming you're in sunny Apulia.

plum and biscotti gelato

The Italians have some of the most civilized habits of any nation. In any piazza in virtually any town the length of the country, you can join the evening passegiata. This ritual of relaxed strolling and chatting is invariably fueled by scoops of pastel-hued gelato—in the south they shamelessly eat it for breakfast, slathered thickly over fresh brioche! Italian gelato is generally milk-based, containing egg and sometimes cream, and always packs an intense punch, whether chocolate or pistachio, lemon, melon, or any flavor under the continental sun. Gelato, which derives from the Italian verb "to freeze," tends to be lower in fat than its ice cream cousins from other corners of the world; it also has less air beaten into it and is stored at a slightly warmer temperature. Hence, the texture is soft and meltingly smooth and, because it is not mouth-numbingly chilled, the taste buds can really revel in its flavors. Another chilly dessert from Italy is semifreddo, meaning "partly cold"—a semifreddo has a gelato base, but whipped cream folded into it stops it freezing completely. Throughout Italy, gelaterias pride themselves on having *Produzione Artigianale* status—which in our language refers to artisanal production, being handcrafted without chemical additives. But of course you can boast this, too, by making any of our recipes at home. The only quandary is what to make. A chinotto and lemon granita, or a classic vanilla gelato? Almond semifreddo, or strawberry balsamic granita? Hmmm, decisions, decisions . . .

chocolate gelato

3 cups milk

1 cup superfine sugar

1/2 teaspoon vanilla extract

1/4 teaspoon instant coffee
granules

1 1/4 cups grated good-quality
dark chocolate

Put the milk, sugar, and vanilla in a saucepan over medium heat. Stirring constantly, cook for a few minutes or until the sugar dissolves and the milk is just about to boil. Remove from the heat and stir in the coffee and chocolate. Continue to stir until the chocolate melts and the mixture is smooth and has a consistent color. Allow to cool slightly, then refrigerate until cold.

Transfer to an ice cream maker and freeze according to manufacturer's instructions. Alternatively, transfer to a shallow metal tray and freeze, whisking every couple of hours until frozen and smooth. Freeze for 5 hours or overnight. Soften in the fridge for 30 minutes before serving.

Makes 4 cups

lemon gelato

2 cups milk

2 tablespoons lemon zest, finely grated

1/2 cup superfine sugar

5 egg yolks

3/4 cup lemon juice

3 tablespoons heavy cream

Put the milk, lemon zest, and half the sugar in a saucepan over medium heat. Stirring constantly, cook for a few minutes or until the sugar dissolves and the milk is just about to boil. Remove from the heat.

Whisk the egg yolks and remaining sugar in a large bowl. Whisk in 1/4 cup of the hot milk mixture until smooth. Whisk in the remaining milk mixture, then return to a clean saucepan and stir constantly over low–medium heat for 8–10 minutes or until the mixture thickens and coats the back of a spoon. Do not allow to boil. Set aside to cool slightly, then cover and refrigerate until cold.

Strain the custard into a bowl, then stir in the lemon juice and cream. Transfer to an ice cream maker and freeze according to manufacturer's instructions. Alternatively, transfer to a shallow metal tray and freeze, whisking every couple of hours until frozen and smooth. Freeze for 5 hours or overnight. Soften in the fridge for 30 minutes before serving.

Makes 4 cups

Walnut toffee satisfies the "inner child," while lashings of walnut liqueur add a sensual slurp of sophistication.

walnut semifreddo

walnut toffee
3/4 cup walnuts, toasted
1/2 cup superfine sugar

2 1/2 cups heavy whipping cream
2 eggs, separated
3/4 cup confectioners' sugar
2 tablespoons Nocello or other walnut liqueur
extra Nocello, for drizzling (optional)

To make the walnut toffee, line a cookie sheet with baking paper and spread the walnuts in an even layer. Put the sugar in a saucepan with 1/3 cup water and stir with a metal spoon over medium heat until the sugar dissolves. Without stirring, bring to a boil and cook for 10 minutes or until dark golden. Carefully pour the mixture over the walnuts and leave for 10–25 minutes or until set. Break the walnut toffee into small pieces, then put in a food processor and finely crush.

Pour the cream into a large bowl and whisk until soft peaks form. Whisk the egg yolks with a quarter of the confectioners' sugar until pale. Whisk the egg whites in a clean, dry glass bowl until stiff peaks form, then gradually add the rest of the confectioners' sugar and whisk again until glossy, stiff peaks form. Gently fold the egg yolks into the cream, then fold in the egg whites. Fold in the crushed walnut toffee and the liqueur.

Line six 1-cup molds with two long strips of foil each. Spoon the mixture into each mold, level the surface, and tap each mold on the countertop a few times to release any air bubbles. Cover with more foil and freeze for at least 24 hours. To remove from the mold, leave at room temperature for 5 minutes, then use the foil strips as handles to lift out the semifreddos and invert onto plates. Drizzle with extra liqueur if desired.

Serves 6

walnut semifreddo

ricotta cannoli semifreddo

1 cup full-cream ricotta cheese, drained of excess liquid (see note)

1/4 cup superfine sugar

1/2 teaspoon lemon zest, finely grated

1/4 cup good-quality dark chocolate, finely chopped

2 tablespoons mixed peel, chopped

1 tablespoon unsalted pistachios, shelled and chopped

3/4 cup light whipping cream

16 cannoli shells

1/4 cup finely chopped good-quality dark chocolate, extra, melted

In a large bowl, beat the ricotta and sugar until smooth. Stir in the lemon zest, chocolate, mixed peel, and pistachios. Beat the cream until soft peaks form, then fold the cream into the ricotta mixture.

Using a palette knife or a teaspoon, fill the cannoli shells with the ricotta mixture. Smooth over the ends and dip one end in the melted chocolate. Place in a single layer on a lined tray, cover with plastic wrap, and freeze for 2 hours or until firm but not too hard. Soften in the fridge for 10 minutes before serving.

Note: Choose a soft ricotta for this recipe.

Serves 6–8

cantaloupe sorbetto

½ cup superfine sugar

2½ cups cantaloupe (or other orange-fleshed melon), puréed

½ teaspoon vanilla extract

1 tablespoon lime juice

2 egg whites

Put the sugar and 1 cup of water in a saucepan over medium heat. Stirring constantly, cook for a few minutes or until the sugar dissolves and the mixture is just about to boil. Set aside to cool.

Pour the sugar syrup into a food processor and add the melon purée, vanilla, lime juice, and egg whites. Blend until smooth, then cover and refrigerate for 2–3 hours or until well chilled.

Transfer to an ice cream maker and freeze according to manufacturer's instructions. Alternatively, transfer to a shallow metal tray and freeze, whisking every couple of hours until frozen and smooth. Freeze for 4 hours or overnight. Store in the freezer until ready to serve.

Serving suggestion: Serve scooped into hollowed-out cantaloupe halves.

Makes 4 cups

Inspire an Italian mood with a batch of fig gelato. Close your eyes, savor several seductive mouthfuls, and you're there!

fresh fig gelato

1 pound (about 6) fresh black figs
1 cup superfine sugar
4 large egg yolks
1$\frac{1}{2}$ tablespoons lemon juice
1$\frac{1}{4}$ cups heavy cream

Cut the stalks off the figs and chop the flesh into quarters, then place in a small saucepan with half the sugar. Stir over low heat to dissolve the sugar. Stirring occasionally, let the mixture simmer gently for 15 minutes. Strain and remove the figs and continue to simmer the liquid over low heat for 10 minutes or until it becomes syrupy. Set aside to cool.

Put the remaining sugar in a small saucepan with 1 cup of water. Stir well to dissolve the sugar. Then, without stirring, bring to a boil and cook for 15 minutes. Every now and then, wipe the inside of the pan with a basting brush dipped in cold water to stop the sugar from crystallizing.

Meanwhile, whisk the egg yolks in a large bowl until pale and creamy. Whisking slowly, gradually beat in the sugar syrup. Scrape the bowl and whisk again to incorporate the ingredients. Some syrup will set on the side of the bowl—don't scrape this into the mixture as it will form lumps.

Roughly chop the cooked figs in a food processor. Add the reserved fig syrup and blend until smooth, then fold into the egg mixture using a spatula. Fold in the lemon juice.

Whisk the cream until soft peaks form. Fold one-third of the cream into the fig mixture, then fold in the remaining cream.

Transfer to an ice cream maker and freeze according to manufacturer's instructions. Alternatively, transfer to a shallow metal tray and freeze, whisking every couple of hours until frozen and smooth. Freeze for 5 hours or overnight. Soften in the fridge for 30 minutes before serving.

Makes 4 cups

fresh fig gelato

cherry sorbetto

1/2 cup superfine sugar
1 pound frozen pitted cherries,
    thawed, juice reserved
1/2 cup apple juice
1/2 teaspoon vanilla extract

1/4 teaspoon almond extract
    (optional)
1 tablespoon lime juice
2 egg whites

Put the sugar and 1/2 cup of water in a saucepan over medium heat. Stirring constantly, cook until the sugar dissolves and the mixture is just about to boil. Set aside to cool.

Blend the cherries and reserved juice in a food processor for 1 minute. Add the sugar syrup, apple juice, vanilla, almond extract, lime juice, and egg whites, then process until combined. Cover and refrigerate for 2–3 hours, until well chilled.

Transfer to an ice cream maker and freeze according to manufacturer's instructions. Alternatively, transfer to a shallow metal tray and freeze, whisking every couple of hours until frozen and smooth. Freeze for 4 hours or overnight. Store in the freezer until ready to serve.

Makes 4 cups

hazelnut gelato

1 cup milk	1/2 cup superfine sugar
1 cup light whipping cream	1/2 cup roasted hazelnuts,
4 tablespoons ground hazelnuts	skinned and chopped
5 large egg yolks	1/4 cup Frangelico

Put the milk, cream, and ground hazelnuts in a saucepan over low heat for 5 minutes, stirring occasionally.

Whisk the egg yolks and sugar in a large bowl. Whisk in 1/4 cup of the hot milk mixture until smooth. Whisk in the remaining milk mixture, then return to a clean saucepan and stir constantly over low–medium heat for 8–10 minutes or until the mixture thickens and coats the back of a spoon. Do not allow the mixture to boil. Stir in the chopped hazelnuts and Frangelico. Set aside to cool slightly, then refrigerate until cold.

Transfer to an ice cream maker and freeze according to manufacturer's instructions. Alternatively, transfer to a shallow metal tray and freeze, whisking every couple of hours until frozen and creamy. Freeze for 5 hours or overnight. Soften in the fridge for 30 minutes before serving.

Makes 4 cups

Frozen zabaglione is the acme of deliciousness—with a drizzle of marsala sauce, it becomes a supreme indulgence.

frozen zabaglione with marsala sauce

2/3 cup light whipping cream
3 egg yolks
1/2 teaspoon vanilla extract
3/4 cup Marsala
1/3 cup superfine sugar

1/3 cup whole blanched
   almonds, toasted and
   chopped
almonds, extra to garnish
   (optional)

Whip the cream to firm peaks, then cover and refrigerate until needed.

Put the egg yolks, vanilla extract, 1/2 cup of the Marsala, and half the sugar in a nonmetallic bowl and whisk well.

Fill a saucepan one-third full of water and bring to a simmer over medium heat. Set the bowl on top of the saucepan, making sure the base of the bowl does not touch the water. Whisk continuously for 5 minutes or until the mixture is thick, foamy, and holds its form when drizzled from the whisk.

Remove the bowl from the heat and place in a bowl of ice. Whisk the mixture for an additional 3 minutes or until cool. Remove from the ice, then gently fold in the whipped cream and toasted almonds. Carefully pour into six $1/2$-cup molds or ramekins, cover with plastic wrap, and freeze for 4 hours or until firm.

Combine the remaining Marsala and sugar in a small saucepan and stir over low heat until the sugar dissolves. Bring just to a boil, then reduce the heat and simmer for 4–5 minutes or until just syrupy—do not overcook or the syrup will harden when cool. Remove from the heat and set aside until needed.

To serve, briefly dip the molds in warm water and loosen with a knife. Turn out onto plates and drizzle with the sauce. Garnish with almonds if desired.

Serves 6

frozen zabaglione with marsala sauce

chinotto and lemon granita

1/4 cup superfine sugar
grated zest of 1 lemon
1³/4 cups Chinotto (Italian cola)
2 teaspoons lemon juice

Put the sugar, lemon zest, and ¹/2 cup of water in a small saucepan and stir over high heat until the sugar dissolves. Bring to a boil, then remove from the heat and allow to cool to room temperature. Refrigerate for 4 hours, until completely cold—the longer the better as this helps the lemon to infuse. Pour into a shallow metal tray and freeze.

Put the Chinotto in a bowl with a pouring lip. Strain the sugar syrup into the bowl and add the lemon juice. Stir to combine, then pour into a shallow tray and freeze for 2¹/2 hours or until the mixture starts to freeze around the edges.

Scrape the frozen edges back into the mixture with a fork. Repeat every 30 minutes for 3 hours or until evenly sized ice crystals form. If you are preparing the granita ahead of time, store it in the freezer and scrape once again just before serving. To serve, scrape into dishes with a fork.

Serves 4–6

semifreddo with caramel oranges

1 1/2 cups heavy whipping cream
9 egg yolks
1 cup superfine sugar
1/3 cup Marsala

grated zest of 2 oranges
2 oranges, peeled, pith
  removed, and sliced
1/2 cup sugar

Whip the cream to firm peaks, then cover and refrigerate until needed.

Combine the egg yolks, sugar, and Marsala in a heatproof bowl over a pan of simmering water, making sure the base of the bowl does not touch the water. Whisk continuously for 5 minutes or until thick and foamy.

Set the bowl in another bowl of ice, whisking for 3 minutes or until cool. Remove from the ice, fold in the whipped cream, and freeze until partially frozen, but still soft. Fold in the zest. Spoon into a bar pan lined with plastic wrap. Freeze for 4 hours or overnight.

Put the orange slices in a glass bowl. Melt the sugar in a small pan over medium heat, tilting the pan from side to side so the sugar caramelizes evenly. Carefully add 1/3 cup of water (it may splatter!), remelt the caramel, and pour it over the oranges. Cover and refrigerate until cold. Serve with slices of the semifreddo.

Serves 8

chocolate tartufo

3 cups milk

1 cup light whipping cream

3/4 cup superfine sugar

1 cup unsweetened cocoa
    powder

1/2 cup good-quality bittersweet
    chocolate, finely chopped

4 large egg yolks

6 chocolate truffles

1 cup good-quality bittersweet
    chocolate, finely shaved

Put the milk, cream, and half the sugar in a saucepan over medium heat. Stirring constantly, cook for a few minutes or until the sugar dissolves and the mixture is just about to boil. Remove from the heat. Add the cocoa powder and finely chopped chocolate and whisk to combine.

Whisk the egg yolks and remaining sugar in a large bowl. Whisk in 1/4 cup of the hot chocolate mixture until smooth. Whisk in the remaining chocolate mixture, then return to a clean saucepan and stir constantly over low–medium heat for 8–10 minutes or until the mixture thickens and coats the back of a spoon. Do not allow to boil. Set aside to cool slightly, then refrigerate until cold.

Transfer to an ice cream maker and freeze according to manufacturer's instructions. Alternatively, transfer to a shallow metal tray and freeze, whisking every couple of hours until frozen and creamy.

To assemble the tartufos, line twelve $1/2$-cup semicircular molds with plastic wrap. Spoon the ice cream into the molds to within $1/4$ inch from the top.

Set a chocolate truffle in the center of each of the six molds, gently pushing them into the ice cream, but leaving the top of the truffles exposed. Freeze all the tartufos for 2 hours.

Carefully lift out the ice cream molds without the truffles. Join them together with the molds containing the truffles, to make six balls.

Freeze for an additional 1–2 hours, then carefully remove the gelato balls from the molds. Roll each ball in the shaved chocolate and serve.

Note: The tartufos can be made in advance and stored in the freezer until ready to serve. Allow to soften in the refrigerator for 1 hour before serving.

Makes 6

chocolate tartufo

chestnut, honey, and fennel gelato

2½ cups milk
1 cup light whipping cream
½ teaspoon vanilla extract
¼ cup superfine sugar
2 teaspoons ground fennel

4 large egg yolks
¼ cup honey
½ cup canned sweetened
   chestnut purée

Put the milk, cream, vanilla extract, sugar, and fennel in a saucepan over medium heat. Stirring constantly, cook for a few minutes or until the sugar dissolves and the milk is just about to boil. Remove from the heat.

Whisk the egg yolks and honey in a large bowl. Whisk in ¼ cup of the hot milk mixture until smooth. Whisk in the remaining milk, then return to a clean saucepan and stir constantly over low–medium heat for 8–10 minutes or until the mixture thickens and coats the back of a spoon. Do not allow to boil. Remove from the heat and whisk in the chestnut purée. Cool slightly, then cover and refrigerate until cold.

Transfer to an ice cream maker and freeze according to manufacturer's instructions. Alternatively, transfer to a shallow metal tray and freeze, whisking every couple of hours until frozen and smooth. Freeze for 5 hours or overnight. Soften in the fridge for 30 minutes before serving.

Makes 4 cups

vanilla gelato

4 cups milk
1 cup superfine sugar
1½ teaspoons vanilla extract

sweet almond bread, gourmet
cookies, or wafers, to serve
(optional)

Put the milk, sugar, and vanilla extract in an ice cream maker and freeze according to manufacturer's instructions.

Alternatively, whisk the milk, sugar, and vanilla extract together in a large bowl until the sugar dissolves, then transfer to a shallow metal tray and freeze, whisking every couple of hours until the gelato is frozen and smooth. Freeze for 4 hours or overnight.

Soften in the fridge for 30 minutes before serving. Scoop into serving glasses and serve with sweet almond bread, cookies, or wafers if desired.

Makes 4 cups

There's a neat trick to this spectacular, cassata-like dessert: you can cheat by using purchased gelato and no one will ever know!

panettone gelato cake

one 2-pound panettone
1 quantity coffee gelato (see page 144) or 4 cups store-bought, softened
1 quantity vanilla gelato (see page 127) or 4 cups store-bought, softened
1/4 cup confectioners' sugar
2 teaspoons ground cinnamon

Cut a slice about 3/4-inch thick off the top of the panettone and set aside. Using a sharp knife, carefully cut around the inside edge of the panettone, about 3/4 inch from the edge. Using this as a guide, hollow out the inside of the cake, down to about 3/4 inch from the base. Put half the cake crumbs into a blender and process to fine bread crumbs (reserve the remaining cake pieces for another use).

Spoon the coffee gelato into the hollowed-out panettone, packing it down and smoothing the top. Sprinkle the cake crumbs over the gelato, pressing them down gently. Wrap the panettone in a large piece of foil and freeze for about 2 hours or until the gelato is frozen.

Spoon the vanilla gelato over the coffee gelato, smooth the surface, and put the lid back on. Wrap in foil and freeze for at least 6 hours.

Remove the panettone from the freezer 30 minutes before serving and place in the fridge to soften slightly. Sift together the confectioners' sugar and cinnamon, then sprinkle over the top of the panettone.

Cut the panettone into wedges (as you would slice a cake) and serve.

Serves 10–12

panettone gelato cake

torrone semifreddo

4 large eggs, separated
$2/3$ cup confectioners' sugar,
   sifted
$1/2$ teaspoon vanilla extract
1 tablespoon honey

1 cup heavy whipping cream
$5^1/2$ ounces torrone (firm Italian
   nougat)

Put the egg yolks, 2 tablespoons of the confectioners' sugar, the vanilla, and honey in a large bowl. Whisk for 5 minutes or until thick and creamy.

In a separate bowl, whisk the egg whites, gradually whisking in the remaining confectioners' sugar 1 tablespoon at a time. Whisk for about 5 minutes or until thick and glossy.

Whisk the cream to soft peaks. Fold one-third of the egg whites into the cream using a spatula, then the rest of the egg whites. Fold one-third of this mixture into the egg yolk mixture, then fold in the remainder.

Chop the torrone into small pieces. Fold the torrone into the semifreddo. Scrape the mixture into a 4-cup container, then cover and freeze overnight. Soften the semifreddo in the refrigerator for 15 minutes before serving.

Serves 6

ruby red grapefruit granita

1/2 cup superfine sugar
11/2 cups ruby red grapefruit
    juice, freshly squeezed
2/3 cup sweet dessert wine

Put the sugar and 1/2 cup of water in a small saucepan and bring to a boil. Reduce the heat and simmer for 3–4 minutes, then remove from the heat and set aside to cool.

Stir the grapefruit juice and dessert wine into the cooled sugar syrup. Pour into a shallow tray and freeze for 21/2 hours or until the mixture starts to freeze around the edges.

Scrape the frozen edges back into the mixture with a fork. Repeat every 30 minutes for about 3 hours or until evenly sized ice crystals form. If you are preparing the granita ahead of time, store it in the freezer and scrape once again just before serving. To serve, scrape into dishes with a fork.

Serves 4–6

Now here's an intelligent idea—chocolate gelato drizzled with liqueur then drowned in coffee. Strictly Adults Only.

chocolate affogato

4 cups milk
1 1/4 cups superfine sugar
1/2 teaspoon vanilla extract
1 1/4 cups good-quality dark chocolate, finely grated
6 small cups of espresso or very strong coffee, freshly made
6 shots Frangelico

Put the milk, sugar, and vanilla extract in a saucepan over medium heat. Stirring constantly, cook for a few minutes or until the sugar dissolves and the milk is just about to boil.

Remove from the heat and stir in the chocolate. Continue to stir until the chocolate melts and the mixture is smooth. Allow to cool slightly, then refrigerate until cold.

Transfer to an ice cream maker and freeze according to manufacturer's instructions. Alternatively, transfer to a shallow metal tray and freeze, whisking every couple of hours until the gelato is frozen and creamy in texture. Freeze for about 5 hours or overnight.

Scoop small balls of gelato out of the container and put them into six coffee cups or heatproof glasses, then put the cups in the freezer briefly while you make the coffee. (You may have a little ice cream left over—enjoy it after your guests have gone!)

Serve the gelato with the Frangelico and coffee poured over it.

Note: This gelato is also delicious drizzled with coffee or chocolate liqueur instead of Frangelico.

Serves 6

chocolate affogato

cinnamon semifreddo

1 cup superfine sugar
4 eggs, separated
2 1/2 cups heavy whipping cream

1 1/2 teaspoons ground
cinnamon

Line a bar pan with a double layer of plastic wrap, allowing the excess to overhang the sides.

Whisk the sugar and egg yolks in a bowl until thick and pale. In a separate bowl, whisk the cream to soft peaks, then gently fold through the egg yolk mixture along with the cinnamon.

In a separate bowl, whisk the egg whites with a pinch of salt until firm peaks form. Gently fold through the egg yolk mixture. Pour into the prepared pan and cover with plastic wrap. Freeze overnight or until firm.

Soften the semifreddo in the refrigerator for 15 minutes before serving. Turn out onto a board, remove the plastic wrap, and cut into slices.

Serving suggestion: This semifreddo is lovely with lightly stewed apples.

Serves 8

nectarine sorbetto

½ cup superfine sugar

2 pounds 4 ounces (about 8)
  ripe nectarines

½ teaspoon vanilla extract

2 egg whites

Put the sugar and 1 cup of water in a saucepan over medium heat. Stirring constantly, cook for a few minutes, until the sugar dissolves and the mixture is just about to boil. Set aside to cool.

To peel the nectarines, score a cross in the base of each one. Put them in a heatproof bowl and cover with boiling water. Leave for 30 seconds, then transfer to cold water and peel the skin away from the cross. Purée the flesh in a food processor until smooth, then add the sugar syrup, vanilla extract, and egg whites. Process until combined. Cover and refrigerate for 2–3 hours, until well chilled.

Transfer to an ice cream maker and freeze according to manufacturer's instructions. Alternatively, transfer to a shallow metal tray and freeze, whisking every couple of hours until frozen and smooth. Freeze for 4 hours or overnight. Store in the freezer until ready to serve.

Makes 4 cups

Think of this elegant dish—with its Italian-flag colors of green, white, and red—as a vibrantly continental salad-in-an-ice.

tomato and basil granita

4 large very ripe tomatoes
1¹/₂ tablespoons superfine sugar
2 cups tomato juice
2 tablespoons basil, finely
  shredded

1 tablespoon chives, finely
  chopped
2 avocados, finely chopped
2 cups yogurt

To peel the tomatoes, score a cross in the base of each tomato. Put them in a heatproof bowl and cover with boiling water. Leave for 30 seconds, then transfer to cold water and peel the skin away from the cross.

Cut the tomatoes in half and scoop out the seeds with a teaspoon. Roughly chop the flesh, then cover and refrigerate until needed.

Put the sugar and ¹/₂ cup of the tomato juice in a small saucepan and stir over low heat until the sugar dissolves. Reduce the heat and simmer for 3–4 minutes, then set aside to cool.

Put the tomatoes in a blender and purée until smooth, then strain through a fine sieve into a bowl. Add the cooled syrup, remaining tomato juice, basil, and a pinch of salt, then mix well to combine. Pour into a shallow tray and freeze for $2^{1}/_{2}$ hours or until the mixture starts to freeze around the edges.

Scrape the frozen edges back into the mixture with a fork. Repeat every 30 minutes for 3 hours or until evenly sized ice crystals form. If you are preparing the granita ahead of time, store it in the freezer and scrape once again just before serving.

Mix the chives through the avocado and divide among six short glasses. Spoon the yogurt over the top and finish with a generous layer of granita.

Serves 6

tomato and basil granita

coffee gelato

3 cups milk
3/4 cup espresso coffee,
    freshly made
3/4 cup superfine sugar

6 egg yolks
2 tablespoons Tia Maria or
    other coffee liqueur

Put the milk, coffee, and half the sugar in a saucepan over medium heat. Stirring constantly, cook for a few minutes or until the sugar dissolves and the milk is just about to boil. Remove from the heat.

Whisk the egg yolks in a large bowl. Whisk in 1/4 cup of the hot milk mixture until smooth. Whisk in the remaining milk mixture, then return to a clean saucepan and stir constantly over low–medium heat for 8–10 minutes or until the mixture thickens and coats the back of a spoon. Do not allow the mixture to boil.

Strain the custard into a bowl and cool over ice. Stir in the Tia Maria. Set aside to cool slightly, then cover and refrigerate until cold.

Transfer to an ice cream maker and freeze according to manufacturer's instructions. Alternatively, transfer to a shallow metal tray and freeze, whisking every couple of hours until frozen and creamy. Freeze for 5 hours or overnight.

Makes 4 cups

blood orange sorbetto

12 blood oranges
3/4 cup confectioners' sugar
2 teaspoons lemon juice

Cut the oranges in half and carefully squeeze out the juice, taking care not to damage the peels. Dissolve the confectioners' sugar in the orange juice.

Transfer to an ice cream maker and freeze according to manufacturer's instructions. Alternatively, transfer to a shallow metal tray and freeze, whisking every couple of hours until the sorbetto is frozen and smooth. Freeze for about 4 hours or overnight.

Meanwhile, scrape the remaining flesh and membrane out of six of the orange halves, to use as serving dishes. Cover the peels with plastic wrap and refrigerate.

Divide the sorbetto among the orange peels and smooth the tops. Freeze for 2 hours, then soften in the fridge for 30 minutes before serving.

Serves 6

A triple-almond whammy involving crunchy amaretti, Amaretto liqueur, and the toasted nut itself to keep utter nutters happy.

amaretti semifreddo

1¼ cups light whipping cream
⅔ cup confectioners' sugar
4 eggs, separated
¼ cup Amaretto
½ cup blanched almonds, toasted and chopped
8 amaretti cookies, crushed
fresh berries or extra Amaretto, to serve

Whip the cream until firm peaks form, then cover and refrigerate.

Line a bar pan with plastic wrap so that it hangs over the two long sides.

Beat the confectioners' sugar and egg yolks in a large bowl until pale and creamy. Whisk the egg whites in a separate bowl until firm peaks form.

Stir the Amaretto, almonds, and crushed cookies into the egg yolk mixture, then carefully fold in the chilled cream and the egg whites until well combined. Carefully pour or spoon the mixture into the lined pan and cover with the overhanging plastic. Freeze for about 4 hours or until frozen but not rock hard.

Serve the semifreddo cut into slices, perhaps with your favorite fresh fruit or a drizzle of Amaretto.

Note: Semifreddo means "partly cold," so if you want to leave it in the freezer overnight, let it soften slightly in the refrigerator for 30 minutes before serving. The semifreddo can also be poured into individual molds or serving dishes before freezing.

Serves 8–10

amaretti semifreddo

cassata

3/4 quantity of chocolate gelato
    (see page 102) or 3 cups
    store-bought, softened
1 day-old sponge cake
1/4 cup Amaretto
1/2 quantity of vanilla gelato
    (see page 127) or 2 cups
    store-bought, softened

2 tablespoons pistachios,
    chopped
2 tablespoons glacé cherries,
    chopped
2 tablespoons chopped candied
    citrus peel
3 teaspoons sugar

Line a bar pan with foil. Put it in the freezer to chill for 3–4 minutes.

Spoon three-quarters of the chocolate gelato around the inside edges of the chilled pan, smoothing carefully to an even thickness. Freeze until firm.

Cut the cake into 1/2-inch cubes and toss lightly in the Amaretto. Put the vanilla gelato in a large bowl and stir in the nuts, cherries, and candied peel, then gently fold in the sponge squares. Spoon the mixture into the center of the frozen chocolate gelato and smooth over the top. Freeze for an additional 3 hours. Turn out of the pan and cut into slices to serve.

Serves 8

pink grapefruit and basil spuma

1 cup superfine sugar
6 large basil leaves, torn
2½ cups pink grapefruit juice, strained
1 egg white

1 tablespoon superfine sugar, extra
⅔ cup sparkling Italian white wine
small basil leaves, to garnish

Put the sugar and 1 cup of water in a saucepan over medium heat, stirring until the sugar dissolves. Add the basil, cover, and simmer for 5 minutes. Remove from the heat, keep covered, and set aside for 5 minutes. Pour through a muslin-lined sieve into a bowl. Stir in the grapefruit juice, then cover again and refrigerate for 3 hours, until well chilled.

Transfer to an ice cream maker and freeze according to manufacturer's instructions. Alternatively, transfer to a shallow metal tray and freeze, whisking every couple of hours until frozen and smooth.

Whisk the egg white until white and frothy. Gradually add the extra sugar, whisking until thick and glossy. Fold the egg white through the grapefruit mixture until just combined. Spoon into serving glasses, pour the wine over the top, and garnish with basil leaves. Serve immediately.

Serves 4–6

Some marriages are made in heaven. This celestial combination of peaches and bubbly will have you counting your lucky stars.

bellini sorbetto

2 cups superfine sugar
5 large, ripe peaches
3/4 cup Prosecco or champagne
2 egg whites, lightly beaten
extra peaches and dessert wafers, to serve (optional)

Put the sugar in a large saucepan with 4 cups of water and stir over low heat until the sugar dissolves. Bring to a boil, add the peaches, and simmer for 20 minutes. Remove the peaches with a slotted spoon and leave to cool completely. Reserve 1 cup of the poaching liquid.

Peel the peaches, remove the pits, and cut the flesh into chunks. Purée the flesh in a food processor until smooth, then add the reserved liquid and sparkling wine and process briefly until combined.

Pour the mixture into an ice cream maker and freeze according to manufacturer's instructions. When the sorbetto is almost frozen, add the egg whites and continue churning until frozen.

Alternatively, pour the mixture into a shallow metal tray and freeze for about 2$^1/_2$ hours, or until the mixture is starting to freeze around the edges. Transfer to a large bowl and beat until smooth. Refreeze and repeat this step twice more, adding the egg whites during the final beating. Freeze until ready to serve.

Serve the sorbetto in scoops, with sliced fresh peaches and dessert wafers if desired.

Note: Bellini is a cocktail served at Harry's Bar in Venice. It is made of peach juice and Prosecco, an Italian sparkling wine.

Serves 6

bellini sorbetto

coffee granita

1 cup superfine sugar
5 cups very strong espresso
   coffee

vanilla gelato (see page 127)
   or store-bought, to serve
   (optional)

Put the sugar in a saucepan with 2 tablespoons of hot water and stir over low heat until the sugar dissolves. Simmer for 3 minutes to make a sugar syrup, then add the coffee and stir well.

Pour into a shallow tray and freeze for 2^1/$_2$ hours or until the mixture starts to freeze around the edges.

Scrape the frozen edges back into the mixture with a fork. Repeat every 30 minutes for about 3 hours or until evenly sized ice crystals form. If you are preparing the granita ahead of time, store it in the freezer and scrape once again just before serving.

To serve, scrape the granita into small serving dishes with a fork. Serve with vanilla gelato if desired.

Serves 6

strawberry and balsamic granita

3¹/3 cups strawberries, hulled
¹/4 cup balsamic vinegar
1 cup superfine sugar

Combine the strawberries and vinegar in a glass bowl. Leave for 1 hour, stirring frequently.

Put the sugar and 1¹/2 cups of water in a saucepan over medium heat. Stirring constantly, cook until the sugar dissolves and the mixture is just about to boil. Set aside to cool.

Blend the strawberry and vinegar mixture in a food processor. Add the sugar syrup and process until combined. Pour the mixture through a strainer, pushing down on the fruit to extract as much liquid as possible. Pour into a shallow tray and freeze for 2¹/2 hours or until the mixture starts to freeze around the edges.

Scrape the frozen edges back into the mixture with a fork. Repeat every 30 minutes for 3 hours or until evenly sized ice crystals form. If you are preparing the granita ahead of time, store it in the freezer and scrape once again just before serving. To serve, scrape into dishes with a fork.

Makes 4 cups

tiramisu gelato

1 cup milk	1/4 cup instant coffee granules
1 vanilla bean, split lengthwise and seeds scraped	1/3 cup sweet Marsala
	2 tablespoons coffee liqueur
4 egg yolks	1 1/4 cups heavy whipping cream
2/3 cup superfine sugar	6 savoiardi (ladyfingers)

Put the milk in a saucepan with the vanilla bean and vanilla seeds. Heat over low–medium heat until the milk is just about to boil. Remove from the heat and discard the vanilla bean.

Whisk the egg yolks and sugar until pale and frothy. Whisk in 1/4 cup of the hot milk mixture until smooth. Whisk in the remaining milk mixture, then return to a clean saucepan and stir constantly over low–medium heat for 8–10 minutes or until the mixture thickens and coats the back of a spoon. Do not allow the mixture to boil.

Strain the custard and divide between two freezerproof bowls. Dissolve half the coffee granules in one bowl, and stir the Marsala into the other. Refrigerate both bowls of custard for 30 minutes or until cold.

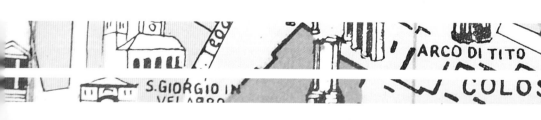

Combine the remaining coffee granules in a small bowl with the liqueur and $1/2$ cup of boiling water. Refrigerate until required.

Whip the cream until soft peaks form. Fold half the cream through the coffee custard, and half through the Marsala custard. Transfer the bowls to the freezer. When the ice cream starts to set, whisk well to break up the ice crystals. Freeze until the ice cream is firm, then beat well again.

Line the base and two long sides of a bar pan with foil and brush with water. Spoon the coffee ice cream into the pan, leveling the surface. Dip both sides of the savoiardi in the chilled coffee liqueur mixture and arrange over the coffee ice cream in a tight layer, trimming them to fit and gently pressing them down. Spoon the Marsala ice cream over the top and level the surface. Cover the pan with foil and freeze until set. Lift the gelato out of the pan, remove the foil, and cut into slices to serve.

159

Alternatively, to prepare the ice cream in an ice cream maker, churn the coffee custard until partly set, then spoon into the pan, top with the coffee-soaked savoiardi, and freeze while you churn the Marsala custard.

Serves 6–8

tiramisu gelato

plum and biscotti gelato

1 pound plums
1/3 cup superfine sugar
dash of almond extract

2 cups good-quality, ready-made
    custard
2 3/4 ounces almond biscotti,
    chopped

Halve the plums, removing the pits. Combine the sugar with 1/2 cup of water in a saucepan and stir over medium–high heat until the sugar dissolves. Bring to a boil, then add the plums and poach for 10 minutes. Set aside to cool.

Purée the plums, poaching liquid, and almond extract until smooth, then stir into the custard. Pour the mixture into an ice cream maker and churn according to manufacturer's instructions until almost frozen.

Alternatively, pour into a shallow plastic tray and freeze for 1–1 1/2 hours or until frozen around the edges but still slushy in the center. Using a hand blender or electric whisk, beat until uniformly slushy. Return to the freezer, beating again at least twice.

Stir in the biscotti and freeze for another 30–60 minutes or until firm.

Makes 4 cups

lime granita

1¼ cups lime juice, strained
    and freshly squeezed
1 tablespoon lime zest
¾ cup superfine sugar

Mix all the ingredients together in a large bowl. Pour into a shallow tray and freeze for 2½ hours or until the mixture starts to freeze around the edges.

Scrape the frozen edges back into the mixture with a fork. Repeat every 30 minutes for about 3 hours or until evenly sized ice crystals form. If you are preparing the granita ahead of time, store it in the freezer and scrape once again just before serving.

To serve, scrape into six chilled glasses with a fork.

Serves 6

vanilla and cinnamon risotto gelato

1 cup milk
1 cup light whipping cream
1/4 cup superfine sugar
1 vanilla bean, split lengthwise and seeds scraped
1 cinnamon stick
3 strips lemon zest
3 large egg yolks
ground cinnamon and finely grated lemon zest, to serve

risotto

1 1/2 cups milk
2 teaspoons grated lemon zest
1/2 vanilla bean, split lengthwise and seeds scraped
1/4 cup superfine sugar
1/4 cup vialone nano or risotto rice
1/2 teaspoon ground cinnamon

Put the milk, cream, sugar, vanilla bean, vanilla seeds, cinnamon, and lemon zest in a saucepan over medium heat. Stirring constantly, cook for a few minutes or until the sugar dissolves and the milk is just about to boil. Remove from the heat.

Whisk the egg yolks in a bowl, then whisk in ¼ cup of the hot milk mixture. Whisk in the remaining milk mixture, then return to a clean saucepan and stir constantly over low–medium heat for 8–10 minutes or until the mixture thickens and coats the back of a spoon. Do not allow to boil. Set aside to cool slightly. Strain through a fine sieve, then cover and refrigerate until cold.

Meanwhile, make the risotto. Put the milk, lemon zest, vanilla bean, vanilla seeds, and sugar in a small saucepan over medium heat. Stirring constantly, cook for a few minutes or until the sugar dissolves and the milk is just about to boil. Stir in the rice and reduce the heat to low. Cover and, stirring frequently, cook for 30 minutes or until the rice is very tender. Remove the vanilla bean and allow to cool slightly. Process half the risotto in a small food processor with ¼ cup of the custard mixture until coarsely chopped, then combine with the remaining risotto and custard. Refrigerate for 2–3 hours or until chilled.

Transfer to an ice cream maker and freeze according to manufacturer's instructions. Alternatively, transfer to a shallow metal tray and freeze, whisking every couple of hours until frozen and creamy. Freeze for 5 hours or overnight. Soften in the fridge for 30 minutes before serving sprinkled with cinnamon and finely grated lemon zest.

Makes 4 cups

vanilla and cinnamon risotto gelato

brandied mascarpone gelato

4 egg yolks
1 1/3 cups confectioners' sugar
2 1/4 cups mascarpone cheese
1 teaspoon lemon zest, very
    finely chopped

1/4 cup brandy
poached pitted fruit and
    almond biscotti, to serve
    (optional)

In a bowl, beat the egg yolks and confectioners' sugar until thick. Gradually beat in the mascarpone until very smooth, then beat in the lemon zest and brandy until well combined.

168

Transfer to an ice cream maker and freeze according to manufacturer's instructions. Alternatively, transfer to a shallow metal tray and freeze, whisking every couple of hours until frozen and creamy. Freeze for 5 hours or overnight.

Soften in the fridge for 30 minutes before serving with poached pitted fruits such as apricots, nectarines, peaches, or plums and almond biscotti, if desired.

Serves 6

olive oil gelato

2½ cups milk
¾ cup light whipping cream
¾ cup superfine sugar
1 large strip lemon zest
8 egg yolks

⅓ cup best-quality, very mild
  and fruity, low-acid Italian
  extra virgin olive oil

Put the milk, cream, sugar, and lemon zest in a saucepan over medium heat. Stirring constantly, cook until the sugar dissolves and the milk is just about to boil. Remove from the heat and discard the lemon zest.

Whisk the egg yolks in a large bowl. Whisk in ¼ cup of the hot milk mixture until smooth. Whisk in the remaining milk mixture, then return to a clean saucepan and stir constantly over low–medium heat until the mixture thickens and coats the back of a spoon. Drizzle in the olive oil in a thin, steady stream, whisking until smooth. Do not allow to boil. Set aside to cool slightly, then cover and refrigerate until cold.

Transfer to an ice cream maker and freeze according to manufacturer's instructions. Alternatively, transfer to a shallow metal tray and freeze, whisking every couple of hours until frozen and smooth. Freeze for 5 hours or overnight. Soften in the fridge for 30 minutes before serving.

Makes 4 cups

Hazelnuts and chocolate are an alluring mix. In cream, they will elicit paroxysms of glee in unsuspecting guests.

chocolate and hazelnut semifreddo

2/3 cup superfine sugar
1/2 cup unsweetened cocoa powder
4 eggs, separated
2 cups light whipping cream
1/4 cup brandy
1/4 cup confectioners' sugar
1 1/4 cups skinned hazelnuts, roughly chopped

Line a bar pan with two long strips of foil. Combine the sugar, cocoa powder, and egg yolks in a bowl. Heat 3/4 cup of the cream in a small saucepan. Stir the hot cream into the egg yolk mixture and blend well.

Pour the mixture back into the saucepan and stir constantly over low–medium heat for 8–10 minutes or until the mixture thickens and coats the back of a spoon. Do not allow to boil. Stir in the brandy and remove from the heat. Allow to cool slightly, then cover and refrigerate until cold.

Whisk the egg whites in a clean, glass bowl until stiff peaks form. In a large bowl, whip the remaining cream to soft peaks. Add the confectioners' sugar to the cream, whipping until stiff and glossy. Lightly fold in the chocolate custard, then the egg whites. Gently fold the hazelnuts through.

Spoon the mixture into the prepared pan, smooth the surface, and wrap the foil over the top to cover. Freeze for at least 24 hours. Leave at room temperature for 5 minutes before serving in slices.

Serving suggestion: The mixture can also be frozen in individual serving-sized ice cream or gelato tubs.

Serves 6

chocolate and hazelnut semifreddo

caramel panna cotta gelato

5 large egg yolks
2/3 cup superfine sugar
2 cups light whipping cream
1 teaspoon vanilla extract

1/3 cup butter
3 tablespoons light whipping
   cream, extra

Beat the egg yolks with half the sugar until thick and pale. Whisk in the cream and vanilla. Pour into a saucepan and stir constantly over low–medium heat for 8–10 minutes or until the mixture thickens and coats the back of a spoon. Do not allow to boil. Cool slightly, then refrigerate until cold.

Transfer to an ice cream maker and freeze according to manufacturer's instructions. Alternatively, transfer to a shallow metal tray and freeze, whisking every couple of hours until frozen and smooth.

Put the butter and remaining sugar in a saucepan and stir over medium heat until the sugar dissolves. Cook for 3–5 minutes, tilting the pan now and then until the mixture turns caramel brown. Remove from the heat and carefully add the extra cream, stirring until smooth. Transfer to a bowl and cool. When the caramel has cooled, transfer the ice cream to a container and swirl the caramel through. Freeze for 4–5 hours or until firm.

Makes 4 cups

chianti sorbetto

1 cup superfine sugar
2/3 cup orange juice, freshly
    squeezed and strained

1 1/2 cups Chianti or light
    red wine

Put the sugar in a saucepan with 1 cup of water. Stir over medium–high heat until the sugar dissolves. Remove from the heat and allow to cool slightly, then stir in the orange juice and red wine. Cool, then cover and refrigerate until well chilled.

Transfer to an ice cream maker and freeze according to manufacturer's instructions. Alternatively, transfer to a shallow metal tray and freeze, whisking every couple of hours until the sorbetto is frozen and smooth. Freeze for 4 hours or overnight. Store in the freezer until ready to serve.

Makes 4 cups

Fresh basil lends its unmistakable spicy edge to this refreshing, sweet ice that begs to be paired with sun-ripened peaches.

basil gelato

1/3 heaped cup superfine sugar
3 teaspoons lemon juice
1 small handful basil
2 cups milk
1 1/4 cups light whipping cream
1/3 cup superfine sugar, extra
6 egg yolks
fresh or poached peaches and pine nuts, to serve (optional)

Put the sugar and 1/3 cup of water in a small saucepan and bring to a boil while stirring. Set aside to cool. Pour into a blender, add the lemon juice and basil, then blend until smooth.

Put the milk, cream, and extra sugar in a saucepan over medium heat. Stirring constantly, cook for a few minutes or until the sugar dissolves and the milk is just about to boil. Remove from the heat.

Whisk the egg yolks in a large bowl. Whisk in ¼ cup of the hot milk mixture until smooth. Whisk in the remaining milk mixture, then return to a clean saucepan and stir constantly over low–medium heat for 8–10 minutes or until the mixture thickens and coats the back of a spoon. Do not allow to boil. Cool slightly, then cover and refrigerate until cold.

Stir the basil syrup into the custard. Transfer to an ice cream maker and freeze according to the manufacturer's instructions. Alternatively, transfer to a shallow metal tray and freeze, whisking every couple of hours until the gelato is frozen and smooth. Freeze for 5 hours or overnight. Soften in the fridge for 30 minutes before serving.

Serve scoops of basil gelato in fresh or poached yellow peach halves with pine nuts sprinkled on top if desired.

Makes 4 cups

basil gelato

roast almond gelato

2/3 cup superfine sugar
1 vanilla bean, split lengthwise
   and seeds scraped
5 egg yolks
2 cups light whipping cream

1/3 cup blanched almonds,
   roasted and chopped

Put the sugar, 2/3 cup water, vanilla bean, and vanilla seeds in a saucepan and stir over low heat until the sugar dissolves. Bring to a boil and cook for 5 minutes. Remove the vanilla bean.

Whisk the egg yolks in a large bowl. Whisk in 1/4 cup of the hot syrup until smooth. Whisk in the cream, then return to a clean saucepan and stir constantly over low–medium heat for 8–10 minutes or until the mixture thickens and coats the back of a spoon. Do not allow to boil. Set aside to cool slightly, then cover and refrigerate until cold.

Transfer to an ice cream maker and freeze according to manufacturer's instructions. Alternatively, transfer to a shallow metal tray and freeze, whisking every couple of hours. When the gelato is half frozen, fold the almonds through. Transfer to a 4-cup container and freeze overnight. Soften in the fridge for 30 minutes before serving.

Makes 4 cups

espresso semifreddo

½ cup ground coffee	4 egg yolks
¾ cup superfine sugar	1 cup heavy cream

Put the coffee, sugar, and ¾ cup water in a saucepan and bring to a boil. Remove from the heat for 3 minutes. Strain through a coffee filter or muslin-lined sieve. Pour back into the rinsed pan and keep warm.

Whisk the egg yolks in a heatproof bowl until pale and light. Whisk in the coffee syrup a little at a time. Put the bowl over a saucepan of simmering water, ensuring the base of the bowl does not touch the water. Stirring, cook until the mixture thickens and coats the back of a spoon. Do not allow the mixture to boil.

Remove from the heat and beat with electric beaters until doubled in volume—the mixture should hold its form when drizzled off the beaters. Cover and refrigerate until cold.

Whip the cream to soft peaks, then fold into the egg mixture. Pour into a bar pan lined with plastic wrap, cover, and freeze for at least 2 hours. Transfer to the fridge for 10 minutes before turning out and slicing.

Serves 4–6

The name rolls off the tongue in dramatic fashion—just watch the jaws drop when this impressive dessert is sighted!

zuccotto

10$\frac{1}{2}$ ounces (1 small) pound cake
$\frac{1}{4}$ cup Maraschino liqueur
$\frac{1}{4}$ cup brandy
$\frac{1}{2}$ cup confectioners' sugar
2 cups heavy cream, whipped
1 cup dark chocolate, chopped
$\frac{1}{3}$ cup blanched almonds
$\frac{1}{4}$ cup hazelnuts, skinned
2 tablespoons chopped candied peel
unsweetened cocoa powder and confectioners' sugar,
    for dusting

Cut the cake into $\frac{1}{2}$-inch slices, then cut each slice into two triangles. Combine the Maraschino liqueur and brandy and sprinkle over the cake.

Line a round, 6-cup bowl with plastic wrap, then the cake slices, pointing the narrow point of each cake triangle into the bottom of the bowl to form a star pattern, and fitting each piece snugly against the others so there are no gaps. Cut smaller triangles to fit the gaps along the top, and keep the rest of the cake for the top.

Add the confectioners' sugar to the whipped cream and whisk until stiff. Mix in about a third of the chocolate and the almonds, hazelnuts, and candied peel, then fill the cake-lined bowl with half the mixture, making a hollow in the middle and drawing the mixture up the sides. Freeze until firm.

Melt the rest of the chocolate in a heatproof bowl over a saucepan of simmering water, then fold it into the remaining cream mixture. Spoon the mixture into the bowl, then cover the top with a layer of cake triangles, leaving no gaps. Cover and freeze overnight.

Remove the zuccotto from the mold 30 minutes before serving and dust the top with alternating layers of cocoa powder and confectioners' sugar.

Serves 6

ice cream truck You may not have a soft-serve dispenser in your kitchen but don't let that stop you from whipping up treats in the spirit of the ice cream man in his merry van. Kids of all sizes jump

with glee when the ice cream truck rolls by, laden with slurpable snowdrifts of soft ice with all the trimmings: crunchy sprinkles, flowing chocolate, and crisp cones in yellow, orange, and pink.

mandarin ice blocks

Ice cream doesn't have too many downsides, except its inability to last outside the freezer for any decent length of time. Melted, it becomes a sloppy, sticky nuisance—which is precisely why the mobile ice cream truck was invented, of course! Beaches, parks, and fairs become infinitely more fun when an ice cream van rolls by, peddling snow cones, Popsicles, and chocolate-studded, candy-sprinkled creations. And then there's that tinkly music and those quaint "Watch that child!" admonishments, not to mention the attendant ice cream truck lore: "The music means he's sold out of ice cream" is a common untruth parents tell their kids as a van chimes and dingles down the street. And no matter how old we might be, we can't help but heed that happy sound with its cheerful associations. Even though most of us these days have a supply of ice cream stashed in our freezers, it remains almost impossible to resist the siren call of the ice cream truck. So any time the whimsy strikes you, flip through this chapter and celebrate the spirit of those funny little vans—go on, indulge your inner child. Be enticed by a pine lime popsicle, or maybe linger over a berry vanilla yogurt popsicle, or throw caution to the wind and dive deep into an extravagant dark chocolate and malt ice cream. Freeze bananas on a stick and dip them in ridiculously rich white chocolate—or serve your own sophisticated take on the classic chocolate-coated cone, impaled with a flaky chocolate bar. It's so easy to recreate that happy carnival atmosphere!

banana ice cream sticks

2 large ripe bananas
1 tablespoon lemon juice
1^1/$_4$ cups ready-made, full-fat custard
^{1}/$_4$ cup milk
6 Popsicle sticks

Put the bananas in a large bowl and mash well until smooth. Stir in the remaining ingredients, mixing well. Pour into a measuring bowl and check that you have about 1^1/$_2$ cups—add a little extra milk if needed.

Spoon into six ^{1}/$_2$-cup Popsicle molds. Push the Popsicle sticks in and freeze for 5–6 hours.

Dip quickly in hot water to remove the molds.

Makes 6 Popsicles

pine lime popsicles

1/3 cup sweetened pineapple juice
1 tablespoon lime juice cordial
1/4 quantity of vanilla ice cream (see page 16) or
    1 cup store-bought
8 Popsicle sticks

Mix together the pineapple juice and cordial. Pour into eight 1/4-cup Popsicle molds and freeze for 3 hours.

Remove from the freezer, then top each one with about 1 1/2 tablespoons of ice cream and press down to compact the ice blocks. Push the Popsicle sticks in and freeze for another 2–4 hours or until frozen.

Dip quickly in hot water to remove the molds.

Makes 8 Popsicles

Elevate the ordinary into the extraordinary by scooping real vanilla bean ice cream into your own handmade cones!

chocolate tops with homemade ice cream cones

ice cream cones
3/4 cup plain all-purpose flour
3/4 cup confectioners' sugar
3/4 cup sour cream
3 tablespoons butter, melted

chocolate topping
3/4 cup good-quality dark
    chocolate, chopped
1/4 cup white vegetable
    shortening

16 small scoops vanilla ice cream
    (see page 16) or store-bought
4 thin, flaky chocolate bars, cut
    in half across the middle

Preheat the oven to 350°F. Mark two 6-inch circles on a sheet of baking paper, then turn it upside down on a cookie sheet.

To make the ice cream cones, sift the flour and confectioners' sugar into a bowl, add the sour cream and butter, and mix until combined. Using a palette knife, spread 1^1/$_2$ tablespoons of the mixture thinly onto each circle. Bake for 8–10 minutes or until starting to turn golden brown. While still hot, wrap each firmly around a conical metal pastry mold, hold in place gently, and allow to cool. When cool, remove the mold. Repeat with the remaining mixture to make eight cones. (For a more even color, put the cones back on the cookie sheet, seam side down, with the molds still inside, and bake for an additional 5 minutes. They may soften again, but will firm on cooling. When cool, remove the molds.) When the cones are cold, store them in an airtight container.

To make the chocolate topping, put the chocolate and shortening in a heatproof bowl and gently melt over a saucepan of simmering water, making sure the base of the bowl doesn't touch the water. Stir until just melted. Remove from the heat and cool to room temperature—if the chocolate mixture is too hot it will melt the ice cream.

Fill each cone with two scoops of ice cream. Make a small hole in the top and insert a chocolate bar portion. Holding the cone over the bowl of chocolate, rotate the cone slightly while pouring chocolate quickly all over the top with a spoon. Allow the excess chocolate to drip off—the chocolate will set very quickly. Freeze for up to 2 hours before eating.

Serves 8

chocolate tops with homemade ice cream cones

passion fruit pavlova ice cream

4 passion fruit
1¹/₂ quantities vanilla ice cream
    (see page 16) or 6 cups
    store-bought, softened
¹/₃ cup coconut, shredded and
    toasted

3¹/₂ ounces ready-made
    meringue nests, broken up
whipped cream, to serve
fresh fruit, to serve
passion fruit pulp, extra to serve

Cut each passion fruit in half and scoop out the pulp—you should have about ¹/₃ cup. Fold the pulp through the softened ice cream along with the coconut and crushed meringues until well combined.

Spoon into a small, lined spring-form cake pan, smoothing the surface. Freeze for 4 hours or until firm.

To serve, turn the ice cream out of the pan, cover with whipped cream, decorate with fresh fruit, and drizzle with extra passion fruit pulp. Cut into wedges as you would a pavlova or cake.

Serves 6

ice cream lamingtons

1 quantity vanilla ice cream
    (see page 16) or 4 cups
    store-bought
4 large savoiardi (ladyfingers)

$1^2/_3$ cups dark or milk chocolate,
    chopped
1 cup shredded coconut,
    lightly toasted

Line a bar pan with baking paper. Allow the ice cream to soften slightly, then spread half the ice cream into the pan. Put the ladyfingers in a single layer over the ice cream, trimming them to fit if necessary, then spread the remaining ice cream over the top. Tap the pan on the countertop to remove any air bubbles, then cover and freeze until firm.

Put the chocolate in a heatproof bowl. Fill a saucepan one-third full of water and bring to a simmer over medium heat. Set the bowl on top of the saucepan, making sure the base of the bowl does not touch the water. Stir the chocolate until melted. Remove from the heat and cool slightly.

Slice the ice cream into six thick squares, then return to the freezer. Set a wire rack over a lined tray. Working one at a time, set an ice cream square on the rack and spoon the melted chocolate over, letting it drip down the sides. Sprinkle toasted coconut all over, then freeze for up to three days.

Makes 6 squares

Who could resist saying okeydokey to a second helping of honeycomb-flecked hokey pokey?

hokey pokey

1¹/₂ cups milk
1 vanilla bean, split lengthwise and seeds scraped
³/₄ cup superfine sugar
4 egg yolks
2 cups light whipping cream
1 cup chopped honeycomb

Put the milk, vanilla bean, vanilla seeds, and sugar in a saucepan over medium heat. Stirring constantly, cook for a few minutes or until the sugar dissolves and the milk is just about to boil. Set aside for 15 minutes to infuse, then gently reheat. Remove from the heat and discard the vanilla bean.

Whisk the egg yolks in a large bowl until well combined. Whisk in ¹/₄ cup of the hot milk mixture until smooth. Whisk in the remaining milk mixture, then return to a clean saucepan and stir constantly over low–medium heat

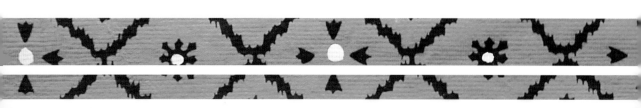

for 8–10 minutes or until the mixture thickens and coats the back of a spoon. Do not allow to boil. Set aside to cool slightly, then cover and refrigerate until cold.

Transfer to an ice cream maker and freeze according to manufacturer's instructions, adding the honeycomb halfway through. Alternatively, transfer to a shallow metal tray and freeze, whisking every couple of hours until frozen and creamy, adding the honeycomb during the final beating. Freeze for about 5 hours or overnight.

Soften the ice cream in the fridge for 30 minutes before serving.

Makes 4 cups

hokey pokey

milk popsicles

1/3 cup superfine sugar
2²/3 cups milk
1 teaspoon vanilla extract
8 Popsicle sticks

Put the sugar and 2 tablespoons water in a small saucepan and stir over low heat until the sugar dissolves. Remove from the heat and set aside to cool. Stir in the milk and vanilla.

Pour into eight ¹/3-cup Popsicle molds. Push the Popsicle sticks in and freeze for 5–6 hours.

Dip quickly in hot water to remove from the molds.

Serves 6

berry vanilla yogurt popsicles

$1/2$ cup strawberries, thinly sliced
$1/2$ cup raspberries
$1/2$ cup blackberries
$1/4$ cup superfine sugar
$1 1/4$ cups thick vanilla yogurt
1 teaspoon lemon juice
6 Popsicle sticks

Put all the berries in a bowl with the sugar. Mix gently and leave to steep for 5 minutes.

If you prefer a chunky-fruit ice block, mash the berries with a fork, then fold in the yogurt, then add the lemon juice. If you prefer a smoother consistency, put the fruit, sugar, and lemon juice in a food processor and blend until smooth. Add the yogurt and blend again.

Pour into six $1/3$-cup Popsicle molds. Push the Popsicle sticks in and freeze for 5–6 hours.

Dip quickly in hot water to remove from the molds.

Serves 6

Food fads come and go but some old classics never die.
This is surely one of them.

chocolate sundae

chocolate fudge sauce
2/3 cup good-quality dark
   chocolate, chopped
3/4 cup sweetened condensed
   milk
1/3 cup light whipping cream
   or milk
3 tablespoons unsalted butter,
   diced

1/4 cup almonds, blanched and
   flaked
1 quantity vanilla ice cream
   (see page 16) or 4 cups
   store-bought
6 glacé cherries
6 wafers

To make the chocolate fudge sauce, put the chocolate, condensed milk, and cream in a heatproof bowl. Fill a saucepan one-third full of water and bring to a simmer over medium heat. Set the bowl on top of the saucepan, making sure the base of the bowl does not touch the water. Stir occasionally until the chocolate has almost melted, then remove from the heat and stir until completely smooth.

Beat in the butter until melted and smooth. Set aside to cool for about 20 minutes, stirring regularly.

Meanwhile, dry-fry the almonds in a frying pan over high heat for 1–2 minutes until light golden, tossing the pan regularly.

To assemble, put two scoops of ice cream into each of six sundae glasses. Pour the chocolate fudge sauce over the ice cream, then sprinkle with the toasted almonds. Top each sundae with a glacé cherry and a wafer and serve immediately.

Serves 6

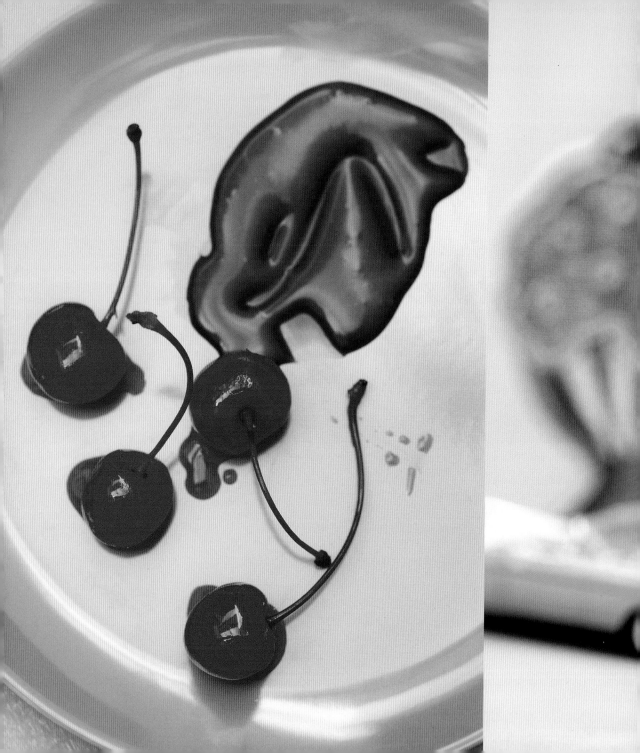

chocolate sundae

mandarin popsicles

2 cups mandarin juice
¹/₂ teaspoon lime zest, finely
   grated

¹/₂ cup canned or fresh
   mandarin segments
8 Popsicle sticks

Combine the mandarin juice and lime zest in a bowl with a pouring lip.

Divide the mandarin segments between eight ¹/₃-cup Popsicle molds. Pour in the mandarin juice. Push the Popsicle sticks in and freeze for 5–6 hours.

Dip quickly in hot water to remove from the molds.

206

Serves 8

chocolate-dipped ice cream balls

½ quantity vanilla ice cream
(see page 16), or 2 cups
store-bought
1 cup each good-quality dark,
white, and milk chocolate

2 tablespoons each chopped
pistachio nuts, toasted
walnuts, and toasted
shredded coconut

Line two large cookie sheets with baking paper and chill in the freezer. Working quickly, use a melon baller to form 36 balls of ice cream and place on the chilled cookie sheets. Stick a toothpick in each ice cream ball. Freeze for 1 hour or until hard.

Put the dark, milk, and white chocolates in three separate heatproof bowls. Bring a saucepan of water to boil, then remove the saucepan from the heat. Position one bowl at a time over the saucepan, making sure the bases of the bowls do not touch the water. Stir occasionally until the chocolate has melted. Remove from the heat and set aside to cool—the chocolate should remain liquid; if it hardens, reheat gently.

Put the nuts and coconut in three separate bowls. One at a time, quickly dip 12 ice cream balls in the dark chocolate, then the walnuts. Freeze. Dip another 12 balls in white chocolate, then the pistachios. Freeze. Dip the last 12 balls in milk chocolate, then the coconut. Freeze for at least 1 hour.

Makes 36 balls

Trap the sunny, juicy flesh of burstingly fresh mangoes within layers of luscious ice cream to savor any time of year.

mango ice cream log

1 cup milk
2 cups light whipping cream
1 vanilla bean, split lengthwise and seeds scraped
$1/2$ cup superfine sugar
6 egg yolks
2 large mangoes, flesh puréed

Put the milk, cream, vanilla beans, vanilla seeds, and sugar in a saucepan. Stirring constantly, cook for a few minutes or until the sugar dissolves and the milk is just about to boil. Remove from the heat. Remove the vanilla bean.

Whisk the egg yolks in a large bowl until well combined. Whisk in $1/4$ cup of the hot milk mixture until smooth. Whisk in the remaining milk mixture, then return to a clean saucepan and stir constantly over low–medium heat for 8–10 minutes or until the mixture thickens and coats the back of a spoon. Do not allow to boil. Set aside to cool slightly, then cover and refrigerate until cold.

Transfer to an ice cream maker and freeze according to manufacturer's instructions. Alternatively, transfer to a shallow metal tray and freeze, whisking every couple of hours until frozen and creamy.

Pack half the ice cream into a bar pan lined with plastic wrap. Refrigerate the remaining mixture until required. Carefully spoon the mango purée over the ice cream and freeze for 2 hours or until firm. Top with the remaining ice cream and freeze overnight.

To serve, briefly dip the base of the pan in hot water, then invert onto a serving plate and cut into slices.

Serves 4–6

mango ice cream log

candied macadamia nut ice cream

2/3 cup macadamia nuts, roasted
1/2 cup superfine sugar
1 quantity vanilla ice cream
    (see page 16) or 4 cups
    store-bought, softened

Put the macadamia nuts on a tray lined with baking paper.

Put the sugar and 1/2 cup water in a saucepan and stir over low heat until the sugar dissolves. Increase the heat to medium and cook for 12 minutes or until it turns deep caramel. Pour it over the nuts and allow to cool and harden. Break into pieces, then put in a food processor and pulse until roughly chopped.

Put the ice cream in a bowl and mix through the candied nuts. Transfer to a 4-cup container and freeze until firm.

Variation: Stir 2 tablespoons of macadamia nut liqueur through the ice cream before freezing, and make extra macadamia toffee shards to serve with the ice cream.

Makes 4 cups

caramel and banana ice cream

3 large ripe bananas
1 1/2 tablespoons lemon juice
1 cup superfine sugar
1 egg

1/4 cup milk
1 3/4 cups light whipping cream
7 ounces soft chewy caramels,
    chopped

Purée the bananas, lemon juice, and sugar in a food processor until smooth. Add the egg, milk, and cream, and process until just combined. Stir through the chopped caramels.

Transfer to an ice cream maker and freeze according to manufacturer's instructions. Alternatively, transfer to a shallow metal tray and freeze, whisking every couple of hours until frozen and creamy. Freeze for 5 hours or overnight. Soften in the fridge for 30 minutes before serving.

Makes 4 cups

Mmmmmm . . . smooth, golden malt adds a gloriously mellow complexion to this deeply chocolate number.

dark chocolate and malt ice cream

1 cup milk
2 cups light whipping cream
1 vanilla bean, split lengthwise
    and seeds scraped
1/2 cup superfine sugar

8 egg yolks
1/3 cup malted milk powder
2/3 cup dark chocolate, melted

Put the milk, cream, vanilla bean, vanilla seeds, and sugar in a saucepan over medium heat. Stirring constantly, cook for a few minutes or until the sugar dissolves and the mixture is just about to boil. Remove from the heat and leave to infuse for 15 minutes. Remove the vanilla bean and gently reheat.

Whisk the egg yolks in a large bowl. Whisk in 1/4 cup of the hot milk mixture until smooth. Whisk in the remaining milk mixture, then divide the mixture between two bowls.

Add the malt to one of the bowls, stirring until well combined. Transfer to a small, clean saucepan and stir constantly over low–medium heat for 8–10 minutes or until the mixture thickens and coats the back of a spoon. Do not allow to boil. Remove from the heat and strain into a bowl. Leave to cool slightly, then cover and refrigerate until chilled.

Repeat this step with the plain custard, stirring the melted chocolate into the strained mixture before chilling.

Pour the cooled malt custard into an ice cream maker and freeze according to the manufacturer's instructions. Alternatively, transfer to a shallow metal tray and freeze, whisking every couple of hours until frozen but still spreadable.

Smooth the malt ice cream into six $2/3$-cup molds and freeze. Repeat the freezing and churning process with the chocolate custard, then spread over the frozen malt ice cream. Freeze until completely frozen.

Serves 6

dark chocolate and malt ice cream

supernatural

1/2 cup dried apricots, finely
  chopped
2 tablespoons currants
2 cups yogurt
1/2 teaspoon vanilla extract
2 tablespoons sesame seeds,
  lightly toasted
1/4 cup dried coconut, lightly

toasted
1/4 cup hazelnuts, roasted,
  skinned, and chopped coarsely
2 tablespoons honey
1/3 cup confectioners' sugar,
  sifted
12 Popsicle sticks

Put the apricots and currants in a small bowl, cover with warm water, and leave to sit for 15 minutes. Drain well. Put all the ingredients in a larger bowl and mix together well.

Transfer to an ice cream maker and freeze according to manufacturer's instructions. Alternatively, transfer to a shallow metal tray and freeze, whisking every couple of hours until almost frozen and creamy.

Divide the mixture among twelve 1/3-cup Popsicle molds and freeze for 5–6 hours or until firm.

Dip quickly in hot water to remove from the molds.

Serves 12

lemonade, lime, and bitters popsicles

1/4 cup superfine sugar
2 1/2 cups lemonade
1/2 cup lime juice cordial

1 teaspoon Angostura Bitters
8 Popsicle sticks

Put the sugar and 1/2 cup of the lemonade in a small saucepan and stir over low heat until the sugar dissolves. Simmer for 3 minutes, then remove from the heat to cool slightly.

Stir in the remaining lemonade, the lime cordial, and the bitters, then set aside to cool completely.

Pour into eight 1/2-cup Popsicle molds. Push the Popsicle sticks in and freeze for 5–6 hours or until firm.

Dip quickly in hot water to remove from the molds.

Serves 8

When the occasion calls for a light finish, serve up some elegant mounds of crushed ice doused in ruby red grape syrup.

red grape snow cones

2 pounds seedless, full-flavored red grapes
$1/2$ cup superfine sugar
$1/2$ teaspoon rosewater (optional)
3 standard ice trays (about 6 cups) of ice cubes

Blend the grapes in a food processor for 1–2 minutes. Pour the mixture through a fine sieve, pushing down on the solids, to make about $2 1/2$ cups of grape juice.

Put the grape juice in a saucepan with 1 cup water and the sugar. Cook over medium heat, stirring constantly until the sugar dissolves. Bring the liquid to a strong simmer and cook for 15 minutes or until slightly syrupy, skimming off any froth if necessary.

Remove the syrup from the heat and stir in the rosewater, if using, and allow to cool—you should have about 3 cups of liquid. Cover and refrigerate for 2–3 hours, until chilled.

Very finely crush the ice cubes in an electric ice crusher or food processor. Alternatively, put them in a plastic bag and crush them with a mallet.

Working quickly, divide the finely crushed ice among six cones or serving glasses, then pour approximately $1/2$ cup of the syrup into each one and serve immediately.

Note: If you prefer the grape syrup to be a little brighter in color, add a few drops of red food coloring until it reaches the desired shade.

Serves 6

red grape snow cones

lemon frozen yogurt

4 cups low-fat vanilla yogurt
3/4 cup lemon juice
3/4 cup superfine sugar
1/4 cup light corn syrup

1 teaspoon lemon zest, finely
  grated
1/2 teaspoon vanilla extract

Put the yogurt in a fine sieve over a bowl and leave to drain in the refrigerator for at least 2 hours. Discard the liquid that drains off.

Put the remaining ingredients in a bowl and whisk together until the sugar dissolves. Add the drained yogurt and whisk well.

Transfer to an ice cream maker and freeze according to manufacturer's instructions. Alternatively, transfer to a shallow metal tray and freeze, whisking every couple of hours until frozen and creamy. Freeze for 5 hours or overnight. Soften in the fridge for 30 minutes before serving.

Makes 4 cups

macadamia and berry parfait

1²/3 cups blueberries
1²/3 cups raspberries
1²/3 cups strawberries
1–2 tablespoons superfine sugar
1/4 cup strawberry or raspberry
    liqueur (optional)

1 quantity vanilla ice cream
    (see page 16) or 4 cups
    store-bought
2/3 cup macadamia nuts, lightly
    toasted and chopped

Combine the blueberries and raspberries in a large bowl.

Hull the strawberries and cut them into halves or into slices if large. Add them to the bowl and sprinkle with enough sugar to balance the tartness of the berries. Pour in the liqueur and gently toss to coat. Cover and refrigerate for at least 2 hours.

Allow the ice cream to soften slightly, then mix the macadamias through. Return to the freezer until firm. To serve, layer scoops of the ice cream and berries in dessert glasses and serve at once.

Serves 6–8

Use a decent, cocoa-rich chocolate here, as real "oomph" is required to round out the flavor of the fragrantly bitter coffee.

mocha ice cream

1/2 cup espresso coffee beans
1 cup milk
3 cups light whipping cream
3/4 cup superfine sugar
6 egg yolks
2 cups good-quality dark
   cooking chocolate, grated

Line a bar pan with plastic wrap and chill. Put the coffee beans, milk, cream, and sugar in a saucepan over medium heat. Stir constantly until the sugar is dissolved and the mixture is just about to boil. Remove from the heat.

Whisk the egg yolks in a large bowl until well combined. Whisk in 1/4 cup of the hot milk mixture until smooth. Whisk in the remaining milk mixture, then return to a clean saucepan and stir constantly over

low–medium heat for 8–10 minutes or until the mixture thickens and coats the back of a spoon. Do not allow to boil.

Strain the mixture to remove the coffee beans, then stir in the grated chocolate until it melts and the mixture is smooth and a consistent color. Set aside to cool slightly, then cover and refrigerate until cold.

Transfer to an ice cream maker and freeze according to manufacturer's instructions. Alternatively, transfer to a shallow metal tray and freeze, whisking every couple of hours until frozen and creamy. Freeze for 5 hours or overnight. Soften in the fridge for 30 minutes before serving.

Serving suggestion: Freeze in a shallow pan until firm, then cut into slices and serve sandwiched between ice cream wafers.

Makes 4 cups

mocha ice cream

chocolate-chip banana ice cream

2 1/2 cups ready-made
   low-fat custard
2 ripe bananas, mashed
2 teaspoons lemon juice

1/3 cup finely chopped
   semisweet chocolate

Put the custard, mashed banana, and lemon juice in a large bowl and mix until no lumps of banana remain.

Transfer to an ice cream maker and freeze according to manufacturer's instructions, adding the chocolate halfway through. Alternatively, transfer to a shallow metal tray and freeze, whisking every couple of hours until frozen and creamy, adding the chocolate during the final beating. Freeze for 5 hours or overnight. Soften in the fridge for 30 minutes before serving.

Makes 4 cups

pineapple sorbet

3²/₃ cups canned unsweetened
    pineapple juice
1²/₃ cups superfine sugar

3 tablespoons freshly squeezed
    lemon juice, strained
1 egg white, lightly beaten

Put the pineapple juice and sugar in a large saucepan over medium heat and stir until the sugar dissolves. Bring to a boil, then reduce the heat and simmer for 5 minutes, skimming off any froth. Cool slightly, then refrigerate until chilled.

Transfer to an ice cream maker and freeze according to manufacturer's instructions, adding the egg white when the sorbet is almost churned and the machine is still running. Alternatively, transfer to a shallow metal tray and freeze, whisking every couple of hours until frozen and smooth, adding the egg white during the final beating. Freeze for 4 hours or overnight. Store in the freezer until ready to serve.

Makes 4 cups

A few basic embellishments—a log shape and chopped honeycomb—turn a simple idea into something grand.

crunchy vanilla ice cream log

1$1/2$ cups milk
1$1/2$ cups light whipping cream
2 vanilla beans, split lengthwise and seeds scraped
$2/3$ cup superfine sugar
8 large egg yolks
2$3/4$ ounces chocolate-coated honeycomb, chopped

Put the milk, cream, vanilla beans, vanilla seeds, and sugar in a saucepan over medium heat. Stirring constantly, cook until the sugar dissolves and the milk is just about to boil. Remove from the heat. Discard the vanilla beans.

Whisk the egg yolks in a large bowl. Whisk in $1/4$ cup of the hot milk mixture until smooth. Whisk in the remaining milk mixture, then return to a clean saucepan and stir constantly over low–medium heat for 8–10 minutes or until the mixture thickens and coats the back of a spoon.

Do not allow to boil. Set aside to cool slightly, then cover and refrigerate until cold.

Transfer to an ice cream maker and freeze according to manufacturer's instructions, adding the honeycomb halfway through. Alternatively, transfer to a shallow metal tray and freeze, whisking every couple of hours until frozen and creamy, adding the honeycomb during the final beating.

Line a large, chilled bar pan with plastic wrap, leaving enough plastic wrap to hang over the long sides. Spoon the ice cream into the pan, pressing down firmly to fill the corners. Smooth the surface, then fold the plastic wrap over the top and freeze for 2 hours. To serve, briefly dip the pan in warm water and lift the log out using the plastic wrap. Cut into 1 1/4-inch slices and serve immediately.

Note: For a layered log, try sandwiching the honeycomb ice cream between layers of chocolate and vanilla ice cream.

Serves 4–6

crunchy vanilla ice cream log

chocolate-coated banana sticks

3/4 cup good-quality white
   chocolate, chopped
6 Popsicle sticks

3 large bananas
1 cup shredded coconut,
   toasted

Put the chocolate in a heatproof bowl. Fill a saucepan one-third full of water and bring to a simmer over medium heat. Set the bowl on top of the saucepan, making sure the base of the bowl does not touch the water, and gently melt the chocolate. Remove the bowl from the heat and stir the chocolate until completely smooth.

Cut the bananas in half across the middle. Push a stick through the cut end of each banana half. Dip the bananas in the melted chocolate to coat, then roll in the toasted coconut.

Put the bananas on a lined tray and freeze for 4 hours or until frozen.

Serves 6

frozen fruit popsicles

1 ripe mango
3/4 cup fresh pineapple, chopped
1 tablespoon mint, chopped
3/4 cup canned, sweetened
    pineapple juice
6 Popsicle sticks

Put the mango, pineapple, mint, and pineapple juice in a blender and blend until smooth.

Pour into twelve 1/3-cup Popsicle molds. Push the Popsicle sticks in and freeze for 5–6 hours.

Dip quickly in hot water to remove from the molds.

Serves 12

Pure genius was at work when this magical mix of chocolate, marshmallow, cherries, and nuts was invented.

rocky road ice cream

1¹/2 cups milk
1¹/2 cups light whipping cream
¹/3 cup superfine sugar
5 eggs, separated
1²/3 cups milk chocolate, finely grated
¹/2 cup dark chocolate, finely chopped

¹/4 cup shredded coconut, toasted
²/3 cup marshmallows, halved
¹/4 cup unsalted peanuts, toasted and chopped
¹/3 cup glacé cherries, halved
²/3 cup good-quality dark chocolate, melted

Put the milk, cream, and sugar in a saucepan over medium heat. Stirring constantly, cook for a few minutes or until the sugar dissolves and the milk is just about to boil. Remove from the heat.

Whisk the egg yolks in a large bowl. Whisk in ¹/4 cup of the hot milk mixture until smooth. Whisk in the remaining milk mixture, then return to a clean saucepan and stir constantly over low–medium heat until the mixture

thickens and coats the back of a spoon. Do not allow to boil. Remove from the heat and stir in the grated milk chocolate until melted, smooth, and consistent in color. Cool slightly, then refrigerate until just chilled.

Transfer to an ice cream maker and freeze according to manufacturer's instructions. Alternatively, transfer to a shallow metal tray and freeze, whisking every couple of hours until frozen and creamy. Freeze for 5 hours or overnight.

Tip the ice cream into a bowl to soften slightly. Quickly stir in the dark chocolate, coconut, marshmallows, peanuts, and cherries and mix well. Pour into a 6-cup bar pan, smooth the surface, cover with plastic wrap, and freeze for 3–4 hours or until firm.

239

To serve, briefly dip the base of the pan in warm water, then invert onto a serving plate. Cut into slices and drizzle with melted chocolate.

Note: For a more exotic version, use white chocolate ice cream (see page 70) and stir through some chopped rose water Turkish delight instead of the chocolate, some toasted pistachios or macadamia nuts instead of the peanuts, and dried cherries instead of the glacé cherries.

Serves 6–8

rocky road ice cream

soda fountain   Like bobby socks and ponytails, rock 'n' roll and blue suede shoes, the soda fountain epitomizes the bubbly, fun-filled 1950s like nothing else. Little is serious (or restrained)

about soda fountain fare, where sundae glasses brim with ice creams covered with gooey sauces, and down-home flavors like blueberry and peanut brittle are the order of the day.

baked alaska

Slowly superseded by the fast food, bottled soft drink, and commercial ice cream proliferation that started in the 1950s, soda fountains were a peculiarly American phenomenon. Drug stores began dispensing artificial mineral waters (the real deal belonged to the filthy rich, who took them for their health). Before long, flavored syrups, scoops of ice cream, and dollops of whipped cream—arguably beneficial to one's mental well-being at least—soon joined the product lineup. As with many finer points of food history, no one knows for certain who first combined ice cream with various sauces, sodas, and toppings, but they certainly started something: their legacy lives on, even though the soda fountain, with its long marble counter, mirrored back wall, goose-necked urns, and squishy-seated, swiveling stools, is pretty much gone. Classic soda fountain offerings included the likes of the Hoboken—a combo of pineapple syrup, milk, soda water, and ice cream. Then there was the CMP, in which ice cream was drowned in chocolate and marshmallow sauces, then showered with chopped, roasted peanuts. Even a chop suey sundae was in the soda fountain lexicon, where a raisin and date syrup, flaked coconut, and—gasp!—chow mein noodles were the distinguishing features. Hot fudge sundaes, coolers, frappés, egg creams, floats, and shakes—served in distinctively retro glasses and dishes—are soda fountain classics; not surprisingly, variations on these themes are still huge favorites today.

banana split

chocolate sauce
1 cup light whipping cream
2 tablespoons butter
2 cups good-quality
   dark chocolate, grated

6 ripe bananas
18 scoops vanilla ice cream (see
   page 16) or store-bought,
   or 6 scoops each of your
   three favorite flavors
chopped nuts and maraschino
   cherries, to serve

Put the cream and butter in a saucepan over medium heat. Stirring constantly, cook for a few minutes or until the butter melts and the cream is just about to boil. Remove from the heat and stir in the chocolate until it has melted.

Split the bananas lengthwise, and put a half along each side of a long glass dish. Set three scoops of ice cream between the bananas and pour the chocolate sauce over the top. Sprinkle chopped nuts over the banana splits, and set a cherry on top.

Serves 6

peanut butter ice cream

2 cups light whipping cream
1 cup milk
1/2 cup confectioners' sugar
6 egg yolks

1/2 cup smooth peanut butter
   (with no added salt or sugar)
1/2 cup sour cream

Put the cream, milk, and confectioners' sugar in a saucepan over medium heat. Stirring constantly, cook for a few minutes or until the sugar dissolves and the cream is just about to boil. Remove from the heat.

Whisk the egg yolks in a large bowl. Whisk in 1/4 cup of the hot cream mixture until smooth. Whisk in the remaining cream mixture, then return to a clean saucepan and stir constantly over low–medium heat for 8–10 minutes or until the mixture thickens and coats the back of a spoon. Do not allow to boil. Remove from the heat.

Thoroughly combine the peanut butter and sour cream and stir into the custard. Cool slightly, then cover and refrigerate until cold. Transfer to an ice cream maker and freeze according to manufacturer's instructions. Alternatively, transfer to a shallow metal tray and freeze, whisking every couple of hours until frozen and creamy. Freeze for 5 hours or overnight.

Makes 4 cups

Here's the ultimate ice cream fantasia: marshmallow, fudgy chocolate, pretzels, and peanuts of every persuasion.

chunky monkey chocolate peanut butter sundae

marshmallow fluff
1 cup white marshmallows
$^{1}/_{3}$ cup light whipping cream

$^{1}/_{2}$ cup chocolate fudge sauce (see page 202)
6 scoops chocolate-chip ice cream (see page 259) or store-bought
$^{1}/_{2}$ cup pretzels, broken up
6 scoops praline ice cream (see page 72)
6 chocolate-coated peanut butter cups, chopped
6 scoops peanut butter ice cream (see page 247) or store-bought
extra chocolate fudge sauce, for drizzling
$^{1}/_{3}$ cup honey-roasted peanuts
chopped chocolate peanut butter cups, extra to serve (optional)

To make the marshmallow fluff, finely chop the marshmallows and melt them together with the cream over low heat until completely dissolved. Allow to cool, then put in the fridge to chill.

To assemble the sundaes, put a tablespoon of chocolate fudge sauce in each of six large sundae glasses. Top each with a scoop of chocolate-chip ice cream, some pretzel pieces, a scoop of praline ice cream, some chopped peanut butter cups, then a scoop of the peanut butter ice cream. Press down to lightly compact.

Add a dollop of marshmallow fluff, drizzle with a little extra chocolate fudge sauce, sprinkle with peanuts, and add peanut butter cups if desired.

Serves 6

chunky monkey chocolate peanut butter sundae

blueberry port sundae

2 cups fresh or frozen
   blueberries
1/2 cup port or muscat
1 cinnamon stick, broken
   in half
1/2 cup superfine sugar

1 tablespoon brandy
1 quantity vanilla ice cream
   (see page 16) or 4 cups
   store-bought
whipped cream, to serve
   (optional)

Put the blueberries, port, and cinnamon in a small saucepan over low heat. Add the sugar to taste, depending on the tartness of the berries. Simmer for 5–8 minutes or until the berries are tender. Remove from the heat and add the brandy. Allow to cool slightly.

Put two scoops of ice cream in each of six sundae glasses. Top with the blueberries and any juices and serve with whipped cream if desired.

Note: The syrup can be served hot or cold over the ice cream. If allowed to cool, the berries will macerate in the port and absorb more flavor.

Serves 6

bourbon and brown sugar ice cream

1 cup milk
$1/2$ cup soft brown sugar
3 large egg yolks

$1/2$ cup bourbon
1 cup light whipping cream

Put the milk and sugar in a saucepan over medium heat. Stirring constantly, cook for a few minutes or until the sugar dissolves and the milk is just about to boil. Remove from the heat.

Whisk the egg yolks in a large bowl. Whisk in $1/4$ cup of the hot milk mixture until smooth. Whisk in the remaining milk mixture, then return to a clean saucepan and stir constantly over low–medium heat for 8–10 minutes or until the mixture thickens and coats the back of a spoon. Do not allow to boil. Strain into a bowl and stir in the bourbon and cream. Set aside to cool slightly, then cover and refrigerate until cold.

Transfer to an ice cream maker and freeze according to manufacturer's instructions. Alternatively, transfer to a shallow metal tray and freeze, whisking every couple of hours until frozen and creamy. Freeze for 5 hours or overnight. Soften in the fridge for 30 minutes before serving.

Makes 4 cups

Texas claims this ice cream as its own—and in true Texan tradition, it is best served in scoops that are larger than life.

butter pecan ice cream

butter pecan sauce
$1/3$ cup maple syrup
$1/3$ cup condensed milk
$1/4$ cup unsalted butter, chopped
$1/4$ cup light whipping cream
$1/2$ cup pecans, roasted and
　　chopped

butter pecan ice cream
$1/2$ cup condensed milk
2 cups light whipping cream
$1/3$ cup milk
$1/3$ cup soft brown sugar
4 egg yolks
1 teaspoon vanilla extract

To make the butter pecan sauce, put the maple syrup and condensed milk in a small saucepan. Stir constantly using a metal spoon over medium–low heat for 8–10 minutes or until golden brown and thickened, taking care not to burn the caramel. Remove from the heat and stir in the butter. The mixture will separate, but comes back together upon stirring. Stir in the cream and pecans and allow to cool completely.

To make the butter pecan ice cream, put the condensed milk, cream, milk, and sugar in a saucepan. Stirring constantly over medium heat, cook for a few minutes or until the sugar dissolves and the mixture is just about to boil. Remove from the heat.

Whisk the egg yolks in a large bowl. Whisk in $1/4$ cup of the hot milk mixture until smooth. Whisk in the remaining milk mixture, then return to a clean saucepan and stir constantly over low–medium heat for 8–10 minutes or until the mixture thickens and coats the back of a spoon. Do not allow the mixture to boil. Stir in the vanilla extract, cool slightly, then cover and refrigerate until cold.

Transfer to an ice cream maker and freeze according to manufacturer's instructions. Alternatively, transfer to a shallow metal tray and freeze, whisking every couple of hours until frozen and creamy. Freeze for 5 hours or overnight.

Spoon dollops of the ice cream into a chilled bar pan and drizzle with the butter pecan sauce. Repeat with the remaining ice cream and sauce to create a rippled effect. Cover and freeze until firm.

Makes 4 cups

butter pecan ice cream

philadelphia-style ice cream

3/4 cup superfine sugar
3¹/2 cups light whipping cream
1/2 cup heavy cream
1 vanilla bean, split lengthwise

Put the sugar in a large bowl with all the cream. Scrape the vanilla seeds into the bowl (reserve the vanilla bean for another use) and whisk until the mixture is well combined and the sugar dissolves.

Transfer to an ice cream maker and freeze according to manufacturer's instructions. Alternatively, transfer to a shallow metal tray and freeze, whisking every couple of hours until frozen and creamy. Freeze for 5 hours or overnight. Soften in the fridge for 30 minutes before serving.

Makes 4 cups

chocolate-chip ice cream

1 cup light whipping cream
1/2 cup milk
1/3 cup superfine sugar
5 egg yolks

1²/3 cups milk chocolate, finely grated
1/2 cup dark chocolate, finely chopped

Put the cream, milk, and sugar in a saucepan over medium heat. Stirring constantly, cook for a few minutes or until the sugar dissolves and the cream is just about to boil. Remove from the heat.

Whisk the egg yolks in a large bowl. Whisk in 1/4 cup of the hot milk mixture until smooth. Whisk in the remaining milk mixture, then return to a clean saucepan and stir constantly over low–medium heat until the mixture thickens and coats the back of a spoon. Do not allow to boil. Remove from the heat and stir in the milk chocolate until melted and smooth. Cool slightly, then cover and refrigerate until cold.

Transfer to an ice cream maker and freeze according to manufacturer's instructions, adding the dark chocolate halfway through. Alternatively, transfer to a shallow metal tray and freeze, whisking every couple of hours until frozen and creamy, adding the chocolate during the final beating. Freeze for 5 hours or overnight. Soften in the fridge for 30 minutes before serving.

Makes 4 cups

chocolate brownie and raspberry ice cream sandwich

8 cups fresh or thawed frozen
raspberries
1^1/$_2$ cups superfine sugar
1^1/$_2$ teaspoons lemon juice
1^1/$_2$ quantities of vanilla ice
cream (see page 16) or
6 cups store-bought,
slightly softened
confectioners' sugar, for
dusting

chocolate brownies
^{2}/$_3$ cup all-purpose flour
^{1}/$_2$ cup unsweetened cocoa
powder
1^2/$_3$ cups superfine sugar
^{2}/$_3$ cup chopped pecans or
walnuts
1^2/$_3$ cups dark chocolate, finely
chopped
1 cup unsalted butter, melted
2 teaspoons vanilla extract
4 eggs, lightly beaten

Line a large square cake pan with baking paper, leaving a generous amount hanging over two opposite sides. Put the raspberries, sugar, and lemon juice in a blender and blend to a smooth purée. Reserving ^{1}/$_2$ cup of the purée, fold the remainder through the ice cream and pour into the prepared pan. Freeze for 2 hours or until firm.

Preheat the oven to 350°F. Lightly grease a 12 x 8-inch cake pan and line with baking paper, leaving the paper hanging over the two long sides.

To make the chocolate brownies, sift the flour and cocoa into a bowl and add the sugar, nuts, and chocolate. Mix together and make a well in the center. Pour the butter into the well, add the vanilla extract and eggs, then mix well. Pour into the pan, smooth the surface, and bake for 45 minutes (the mixture will still be a bit soft in the middle).

Allow the cake to cool a little, then chill for at least 2 hours. Lift it out, using the paper as handles. Trim and cut into twelve $3^1/2$ x 2-inch rectangles then, using a serrated knife, cut through the center of each brownie to form two thinner brownie pieces.

Remove the ice cream from the freezer, using the overhanging paper to lift it from the pan. Cut into 12 rectangles the same size as the brownies.

To assemble, put 12 brownie slices on a tray. Top each with a rectangle of ice cream and then another slice of brownie, placing it cut side down. Smooth the sides of the ice cream to neaten the "sandwich," if necessary. Freeze for 10 minutes to firm. Dust with confectioners' sugar and serve with the reserved raspberry sauce.

Makes 12 sandwiches

chocolate brownie and raspberry ice cream sandwich

coffee, rum, and walnut ice cream

3/4 cup superfine sugar

3 teaspoons instant coffee
  granules

3 cups light whipping cream

1 cup milk

2 tablespoons rum

1/2 cup toasted walnuts,
  roughly chopped

chopped walnuts, extra
  to serve (optional)

Put the sugar, coffee granules, and 1/4 cup water in a saucepan. Stirring constantly, cook for a few minutes or until the sugar and coffee dissolve. Remove from the heat and leave to cool.

In a large bowl, lightly whip the cream. Fold in the cooled coffee mixture and the milk, mixing well.

Transfer to an ice cream maker in batches and freeze according to manufacturer's instructions, adding the rum and walnuts halfway through. Alternatively, transfer to a shallow metal tray and freeze, whisking every couple of hours until frozen and creamy. Add the rum and walnuts during the final beating. Freeze for 5 hours or overnight.

Soften in the fridge for 30 minutes before serving. Serve sprinkled with extra walnuts if desired.

Makes 6 cups

cheesecake ice cream

5 egg yolks
1/3 cup superfine sugar
1 cup milk
1 cup light whipping cream
1 cup cream cheese, softened

1 teaspoon lemon zest, finely
  grated
5 sweet plain cookies, coarsely
  crushed

Whisk the egg yolks and sugar in a large bowl until well combined. Whisk in 1/4 cup of the milk until smooth. Whisk in the remaining milk and cream, then return to a clean saucepan and stir constantly over low–medium heat for 8–10 minutes or until the mixture thickens and coats the back of a spoon. Do not allow to boil. Set aside to cool slightly.

Using electric beaters on high, beat the cream cheese and lemon zest with half the custard for 5 minutes or until very smooth. Beat in the remaining custard, then refrigerate until cool.

Transfer to an ice cream maker and freeze according to manufacturer's instructions, adding the cookies halfway through. Alternatively, transfer to a shallow metal tray and freeze, whisking every couple of hours until frozen and creamy, adding the cookies during the final beating. Freeze for 5 hours or overnight. Soften in the fridge for 30 minutes before serving.

Makes 4 cups

To refine a soda fountain staple, peanut brittle is spiked with coffee and chocolate, then whipped into an airy parfait.

peanut brittle parfait bar

1¹/2 cups superfine sugar
2 cups milk
6 egg yolks
1 tablespoon instant coffee powder, dissolved in 1 teapoon water
2¹/2 cups light whipping cream
4¹/4 ounces chocolate-coated peanut brittle, roughly chopped

Put 1 cup of the sugar and 1/3 cup water in a saucepan over low heat. Stirring constantly, cook for a few minutes until the sugar dissolves, brushing down the side of the pan with a basting brush dipped in water to dissolve the sugar crystals.

Bring to a boil, then reduce the heat and simmer without stirring for 4 minutes or until pale caramel. Remove from the heat and allow to cool slightly, then carefully stir in the milk (the mixture will splatter). Return to the heat and stir until the toffee dissolves. Set aside.

Whisk the egg yolks and remaining sugar in a large bowl until well combined. Whisk in the dissolved coffee and 1/4 cup of the hot milk mixture until smooth. Whisk in the remaining milk mixture, then return to a clean saucepan and stir constantly over low–medium heat for 8–10 minutes or until the mixture thickens and coats the back of a spoon. Do not allow to boil. Set aside to cool slightly, then stir in the cream. Cover and refrigerate until cold.

Pour into a shallow pan and freeze until just firm. Transfer to a large bowl. Using electric beaters, beat until light and fluffy, then return to the pan and freeze until just firm. Repeat the beating process twice more.

Line a large bar pan with plastic wrap. Fold the chopped peanut brittle through the parfait and spread the mixture into the prepared pan. Smooth the surface, cover with baking paper, then freeze until firm. Invert onto a plate and cut into slices to serve. Decorate with toffee shards or peanut brittle if desired.

Serves 8

peanut brittle parfait bar

big peach sundae

candied pecans
1/4 cup superfine sugar
2/3 cup pecans, chopped

1/2 cup light whipping cream
1 large can of sliced peaches
2 teaspoons superfine sugar
2 teaspoons orange-flavored
   liqueur or orange juice

half a 41/2-ounce packet of
   Amaretti cookies, crushed
1 quantity vanilla ice cream
   (see page 16) or cinnamon
   and maple syrup ice cream
   (see page 295)

To make the candied pecans, put a frying pan over medium heat and sprinkle half the sugar over the base. As the sugar melts, sprinkle with the remaining sugar. Stir gently until all the sugar dissolves and is golden brown. Remove from the heat, stir in the pecans, and spread on a tray lined with baking paper to cool. When cold, crush into small chunks.

Lightly whip the cream and set aside. Purée half the peaches with the sugar and liqueur until smooth. Divide the cookies among six large sundae glasses and drizzle with some peach purée. Top with the remaining peaches and scoops of ice cream. Drizzle with the remaining peach purée, add a dollop of whipped cream, and sprinkle with candied pecans.

Serves 6

cosmopolitan float

1¹/4 cups superfine sugar

2 cups strained pink grapefruit juice

¹/2 cup vodka

1¹/4 cups cranberry juice

Put the sugar and 1¹/4 cups water in a saucepan over low heat. Stirring constantly, cook for a few minutes or until the sugar dissolves. Increase the heat to medium and cook for 5 minutes. Remove from the heat, cool slightly, then cover and refrigerate until cold.

Mix the grapefruit juice and vodka into the chilled syrup, then transfer to an ice cream maker and freeze according to manufacturer's instructions. Alternatively, transfer to a shallow metal tray and freeze, whisking every couple of hours until the sorbet is frozen and smooth. Freeze for 5 hours or overnight.

To serve, pour the cranberry juice into six small martini glasses and add two scoops of sorbet to each.

Serves 6

A modern spin on a comfort-food classic results in a buttery-smooth ice cream loaded with strawberry kisses.

strawberry shortcake ice cream

1 cup milk
1 vanilla bean, split lengthwise and seeds scraped
$2/3$ cup superfine sugar
4 egg yolks
$1^{1}/_{4}$ cups mascarpone cheese
$3^{1}/_{3}$ cups strawberries, hulled
5 shortbread cookies, coarsely crumbled
chopped strawberries, extra to serve

Put the milk, vanilla bean, vanilla seeds, and sugar in a saucepan over medium heat. Stirring constantly, cook for a few minutes or until the sugar dissolves and the milk is just about to boil. Remove from the heat. Remove the vanilla bean.

Whisk the egg yolks in a large bowl, then whisk in $^{1}/_{4}$ cup of the hot milk mixture. Whisk in the remaining milk mixture, then return to a clean

saucepan and stir constantly over low–medium heat for 8–10 minutes or until the mixture thickens and coats the back of a spoon. Do not allow to boil. Set aside to cool slightly, then whisk in the mascarpone until smooth. Allow to cool, then cover and refrigerate until cold.

Meanwhile, purée the strawberries in a food processor or blender, then transfer to a heavy-based saucepan and simmer over low heat, stirring frequently until reduced by half. Remove from the heat and allow to cool, then stir into the custard mixture.

Transfer to an ice cream maker and freeze according to manufacturer's instructions, adding the crumbled shortbread halfway through. Alternatively, transfer to a shallow metal tray and freeze, whisking every couple of hours until frozen and creamy, adding the shortbread during the final beating. Freeze for 5 hours or overnight. Soften in the fridge for 30 minutes before serving with extra strawberries.

Makes 4 cups

strawberry shortcake ice cream

pink peppermint candy cane ice cream

2 cups milk
2 cups light whipping cream
2/3 cup superfine sugar

7 ounces mini peppermint candy
    canes, coarsely crushed
4 egg yolks

Put the milk, cream, sugar, and half the crushed candy in a saucepan over medium heat. Stirring constantly, cook until the sugar and candy dissolve and the milk is just about to boil. Remove from the heat.

Whisk the egg yolks in a large bowl. Whisk in $1/4$ cup of the hot milk mixture until smooth. Whisk in the remaining milk mixture, then return to a clean saucepan and stir constantly over low–medium heat for 8–10 minutes or until the mixture thickens and coats the back of a spoon. Do not allow to boil. Cool slightly, then refrigerate until cold.

Transfer to an ice cream maker and freeze according to manufacturer's instructions, adding the remaining crushed candy halfway through. Alternatively, transfer to a shallow metal tray and freeze, whisking every couple of hours until frozen and creamy, adding the crushed candy during the final beating. Freeze for 5 hours or overnight.

Makes 4 cups

ice cream christmas pudding

1/3 cup toasted almonds, chopped
1/4 cup mixed peel
1/2 cup raisins
1/2 cup golden raisins
1/3 cup currants
1/3 cup rum
1 quantity vanilla ice cream
  (see page 16) or 4 cups
  store-bought, softened

1/2 cup green and red glacé
  cherries, quartered
1 teaspoon mixed pumpkin pie
  spice
1 teaspoon ground cinnamon
1/2 teaspoon ground nutmeg
1 quantity chocolate ice cream
  (see page 28) or 4 cups
  store-bought, softened

Mix the almonds, mixed peel, raisins, golden raisins, currants, and rum together in a bowl. Cover and leave overnight.

Mix the glacé cherries into the vanilla ice cream. Working quickly, press the ice cream around the inside of a chilled 8-cup dessert bowl, spreading evenly over the base and up the side. Freeze overnight, smoothing out the hollow several times.

Mix together the remaining ingredients. Spoon into the dessert bowl, smooth the top, and freeze overnight. Invert onto a chilled serving plate and refrigerate for 30 minutes to soften slightly. Cut into wedges to serve.

Serves 10

What could be more American than pumpkin pie? Here it adds a Cinderella touch to regular ice cream.

pumpkin pie ice cream

1 pound 2 ounces pumpkin,
    peeled and chopped
light vegetable oil, for
    brushing
1 1/2 teaspoons ground
    cinnamon
1 teaspoon ground ginger
1/2 teaspoon nutmeg, freshly
    grated

1/8 teaspoon ground cloves
1 cup milk
1 1/2 cups light whipping cream
1/2 cup maple syrup
1/4 cup soft brown sugar
7 egg yolks

Preheat the oven to 325°F. Brush the pumpkin very lightly with vegetable oil and put in a roasting pan. Bake for 40 minutes or until the pumpkin is soft, but do not allow to brown.

Purée the pumpkin while still warm and add the cinnamon, ginger, nutmeg, and cloves. Set aside to cool.

Put the milk, cream, maple syrup, and sugar in a saucepan over medium heat. Stirring constantly, cook for a few minutes or until the sugar dissolves and the mixture is just about to boil. Remove from the heat.

Whisk the egg yolks in a large bowl until well combined. Whisk in $1/4$ cup of the hot milk mixture until smooth. Whisk in the remaining milk mixture, then return to a clean saucepan and stir constantly over low–medium heat for 8–10 minutes or until the mixture thickens and coats the back of a spoon. Do not allow to boil. Set aside to cool slightly, then refrigerate until cold.

Stir the puréed pumpkin into the custard and mix well. Transfer to an ice cream maker and freeze according to manufacturer's instructions. Alternatively, transfer to a shallow metal tray and freeze, whisking every couple of hours until frozen and creamy. Freeze for 5 hours or overnight. Soften in the fridge for 30 minutes before serving.

Makes 4 cups

pumpkin pie ice cream

blueberry ice cream pie

10 plain sweet cookies
$^1/_2$ cup butter, melted
1$^2/_3$ cups fresh or thawed frozen blueberries
1$^1/_2$ quantities of berry ice cream (made with blueberries;
   see page 95), or 6 cups store-bought, softened
1$^1/_3$ cups fresh blueberries, extra

Line the base of an 8-inch round spring-form cake pan with baking paper. Blend the cookies in a food processor until crumbly. Add the melted butter and mix well, then press firmly into the base and side of the pan. Sprinkle the fresh or frozen blueberries over the base.

Dollop the softened ice cream carefully over the berries until the base is covered, then smooth the surface. Tap the pan lightly to remove any air bubbles. Sprinkle the extra blueberries over the top, pressing them lightly into the ice cream. Freeze for 1–2 hours or until firm.

Serves 6

maple yogurt ice cream

3/4 cup maple syrup
6 egg yolks
3 cups vanilla yogurt

Put the maple syrup in a saucepan over medium heat. Stirring, cook for several minutes or until thickened slightly. Remove from the heat.

Whisk the egg yolks in a large bowl until well combined. Add the hot maple syrup in a thin stream, beating well. Continue whisking until cool, then whisk in the yogurt.

Transfer to an ice cream maker and freeze according to manufacturer's instructions. Alternatively, transfer to a shallow metal tray and freeze, whisking every couple of hours until frozen and creamy. Freeze for about 5 hours or overnight. Soften in the fridge for 30 minutes before serving.

Makes 4 cups

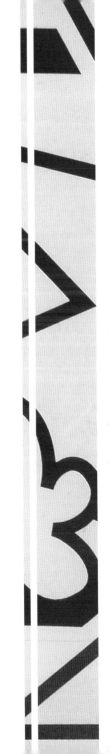

If your dinner party's been a disaster, this spectacular melange
of fruits, nougat, and pistachios will blow everyone away!

tutti-frutti bombe

1 large mango, finely chopped
1 cup canned pineapple pieces,
    drained
1/4 cup Grand Marnier
1 2/3 cups strawberries, puréed
1 3/4 cups condensed milk
2 1/2 cups light whipping cream
2 3/4 ounces nougat, chopped
1/4 cup roughly chopped, shelled
    unsalted pistachios

halved strawberries, extra
    to serve
chopped nougat, extra to serve

toffee bark (optional)
1/3 cup superfine sugar

Lightly grease an 8-cup dessert bowl and line with plastic wrap, allowing
it to hang over the sides. Store in the freezer until ready to use. Drain the
mango and pineapple in a sieve.

Mix the Grand Marnier, strawberry purée, and condensed milk in a large bowl. Whip the cream to soft peaks, then add to the strawberry mixture and whisk until thick. Fold in the drained fruits, nougat, and pistachios. Pour the mixture into the dessert bowl, cover with plastic wrap, and freeze overnight or until firm.

To make the toffee bark, heat the sugar over low heat in a heavy-based saucepan for 2–3 minutes or until melted and golden. Carefully pour onto a cookie sheet lined with baking paper. Tilt the tray to get a thin, even layer of toffee and allow to cool slightly. While still pliable, drape the paper over a rolling pin and allow to cool for 30–60 seconds before peeling away strips of toffee in large irregular shapes. Cool.

Invert the pudding onto a chilled serving plate. Remove the bowl (leave the plastic), and refrigerate for 30 minutes to soften slightly. Remove the plastic and decorate the bombe with toffee bark, strawberries, and nougat.

Serves 8

tutti-frutti bombe

cookies and cream ice cream

1 1/2 cups milk
1 1/2 cups light whipping cream
1/4 cup superfine sugar
6 egg yolks

6 cream-filled dark chocolate
cookies, crushed

Put the milk, cream, and sugar in a saucepan over medium heat. Stirring constantly, cook for a few minutes or until the sugar dissolves and the milk is just about to boil. Remove from the heat.

Whisk the egg yolks in a large bowl. Whisk in 1/4 cup of the hot milk mixture until smooth. Whisk in the remaining milk mixture, then return to a clean saucepan and stir constantly over low–medium heat for 8–10 minutes or until the mixture thickens and coats the back of a spoon. Do not allow to boil. Cool slightly, then cover and refrigerate until cold.

Transfer to an ice cream maker and freeze according to manufacturer's instructions, adding the cookies halfway through. Alternatively, transfer to a shallow metal tray and freeze, whisking every couple of hours until frozen and creamy, adding the cookies during the final beating. Freeze for 5 hours or overnight. Soften in the fridge for 30 minutes before serving.

Makes 4 cups

spiced cherry brandy sundae

1/4 cup superfine sugar
2 tablespoons soft brown sugar
1 teaspoon allspice
1/4 cup brandy
1 pound 2 ounces pitted fresh
   cherries

1 quantity vanilla ice cream
   (see page 16) or 4 cups
   store-bought
brandy snaps, to serve (optional)

Put the sugar, allspice, and brandy in a saucepan with 1 cup of water. Cook over medium heat, stirring constantly, for several minutes or until the sugar dissolves.

Bring to a boil, add the cherries, then reduce the heat to low. Simmer for 10 minutes, then remove from the heat and set aside to cool.

Layer the cherries and ice cream in six sundae glasses and drizzle with any remaining cherry syrup. Serve with brandy snaps, if desired.

Serves 6

vanilla and caramel swirl ice cream pie

12 plain chocolate cookies
$2/3$ cup unsalted butter, melted
1 cup milk
2 cups light whipping cream
1 vanilla bean, split lengthwise
    and seeds scraped
$3/4$ cup superfine sugar
6 egg yolks

caramel
$1/2$ cup superfine sugar
$1/4$ cup light whipping cream
$2^{1}/2$ tablespoons unsalted butter

Lightly grease a $10^{3}/4$ x 6-inch pie dish. Finely crush the cookies in a food processor. Mix in the butter until well combined. Spoon the mixture into the dish, pressing evenly and firmly over the base and sides. Refrigerate until needed.

Put the milk, cream, vanilla bean, vanilla seeds, and sugar in a saucepan over medium heat. Stirring constantly, cook for a few minutes or until the sugar dissolves and the mixture is just about to boil. Remove from the heat. Remove the vanilla bean.

Whisk the egg yolks in a large bowl until well combined. Whisk in $1/4$ cup of the hot milk mixture until smooth. Whisk in the remaining milk mixture, then return to a clean saucepan and stir constantly over low–medium heat for 8–10 minutes or until the mixture thickens and coats the back of a spoon. Do not allow to boil. Strain into a bowl, then cover and refrigerate until cold.

Transfer to an ice cream maker and freeze according to manufacturer's instructions. Alternatively, transfer to a shallow metal tray and freeze, whisking every couple of hours until frozen and creamy. Smooth the mixture into the pie dish and cover with baking paper. Return to the freezer.

To make the caramel, put the sugar in a small saucepan with 1 tablespoon water. Stir over low heat until the sugar dissolves, brushing down the sides of the pan with a basting brush dipped in cold water to dissolve the sugar crystals. Bring to a boil, reduce the heat, and simmer without stirring for 4 minutes or until a pale caramel. Remove from the heat and gradually add the cream, butter, and another tablespoon of water.

Bring to a boil for 5 minutes, stirring occasionally. Remove and cool for 20 minutes. While still slightly warm, swirl the caramel over the pie, then freeze until hard. Cut into slices and serve with any remaining caramel.

Serves 6–8

vanilla and caramel swirl ice cream pie

apple pie ice cream

1 cup canned pie apples
1/2 cup superfine sugar
1 teaspoon vanilla extract
1/4 teaspoon ground cinnamon
good pinch of ground nutmeg
1 cup ready-made custard

1 1/4 cups light whipping cream
5 shortbread cookies, crumbled

Purée half the apple with the sugar, vanilla, cinnamon, and nutmeg until smooth. Then stir into the custard. Lightly whip the cream to soft peaks and fold into the apple mixture. Finely chop the remaining apple and reserve.

Transfer the mixture to an ice cream maker and freeze according to manufacturer's instructions, adding the chopped apple and crumbled shortbread halfway through. Alternatively, transfer to a shallow metal tray and freeze, whisking every couple of hours until frozen and creamy, adding the apple and shortbread during the final beating. Freeze for 5 hours or overnight. Soften in the fridge for 30 minutes before serving.

Note: If the shortbread is very pale, briefly bake in a preheated 350°F oven until golden. Allow to cool before using.

Makes 4 cups

cinnamon and maple syrup ice cream

2 cups milk	2 cinnamon sticks
1/2 cup maple syrup	8 large egg yolks
1 1/2 cups light whipping cream	1 teaspoon ground cinnamon

Put the milk, maple syrup, cream, and cinnamon sticks in a saucepan over medium heat. Stirring constantly, cook for a few minutes or until the sugar dissolves and the milk is just about to boil. Remove from the heat and infuse for 15 minutes. Remove the cinnamon sticks and gently reheat.

Whisk the egg yolks in a large bowl. Whisk in 1/4 cup of the hot milk mixture until smooth. Whisk in the remaining milk mixture, then return to a clean saucepan and stir constantly over low–medium heat for 8–10 minutes or until the mixture thickens and coats the back of a spoon. Do not allow to boil. Add the ground cinnamon and whisk. Set aside to cool slightly, then refrigerate until cold.

Transfer to an ice cream maker and freeze according to manufacturer's instructions. Alternatively, transfer to a shallow metal tray and freeze, whisking every couple of hours until frozen and creamy. Freeze for 5 hours or overnight. Soften in the fridge for 30 minutes before serving.

Makes 4 cups

We all know how great dark chocolate is, but sometimes, only the retro goodness of the milk variety will do.

milk chocolate and pecan ice cream

1 cup milk
1 vanilla bean, split lengthwise
    and seeds scraped
2 cups light whipping cream
1/2 cup superfine sugar
11/2 cups good-quality milk
    chocolate, grated

4 egg yolks
1/2 cup pecans, chopped
grated milk chocolate, extra
    to serve

Put the milk, vanilla bean, and vanilla seeds into a heavy-based saucepan over medium heat. Add 1/2 cup of the cream and cook, stirring constantly, for a few minutes or until the milk is just about to boil. Reduce the heat, add the sugar and grated chocolate, and stir until smooth. Remove from the heat. Discard the vanilla bean.

Whisk the egg yolks in a large bowl until well combined. Whisk in 1/4 cup of the hot milk mixture until smooth. Whisk in the remaining milk mixture, then return to a clean saucepan and stir constantly over low–medium heat for 8–10 minutes or until the mixture thickens and coats the back of a spoon. Do not allow to boil. Set aside to cool slightly, then cover and refrigerate until cold.

Whip the remaining cream to soft peaks, then fold through the custard. Transfer to an ice cream maker and freeze according to manufacturer's instructions, adding the pecans halfway through. Alternatively, transfer to a shallow metal tray and freeze, whisking every couple of hours until frozen and creamy, adding the pecans during the final beating. Freeze for about 5 hours or overnight. Soften in the fridge for 30 minutes before serving.

To serve, scoop the ice cream into serving bowls and sprinkle with extra grated chocolate.

Makes 4 cups

milk chocolate and pecan ice cream

triple chocolate terrine

6 eggs, separated
3/4 cup confectioners' sugar
1 cup good-quality milk
  chocolate, melted
1/4 cup unsalted butter, melted
2 cups light whipping cream,
  whipped into soft peaks

1 cup good-quality white
  chocolate, melted
2 teaspoons instant coffee
  granules, dissolved in
  1 tablespoon hot water
1 tablespoon dark rum
1 cup good-quality dark
  chocolate, melted

Line a bar pan with baking paper, letting it hang over the sides. Beat two egg whites until soft peaks form. Gradually beat in one-third of the confectioners' sugar until thick and glossy. Beat in two egg yolks and the cooled milk chocolate, then a third of the melted butter. Fold in a third of the whipped cream. Spoon into the pan, with the pan tilted lengthwise on its side. Store in the freezer on this angle for 1–2 hours, until just firm.

Repeat the process with the white chocolate, using the same ingredients as before. Spoon into the other side of the pan so the terrine is level, then put the pan flat in the freezer to set. Repeat with the dark chocolate, using up the remaining ingredients. Spoon into the pan, smooth the top, and freeze until firm. Turn out onto a plate and cut into thin slices to serve.

Serves 8–10

raspberry ripple ice cream

1²/3 cups raspberries
1 cup light whipping cream
1 quantity vanilla ice cream
    (see page 16) or 4 cups
    store-bought, softened

raspberries, extra for serving

Blend the raspberries in a food processor until quite smooth. Push the purée through a fine sieve to remove the seeds.

Lightly whip the cream to soft peaks. Using a metal spoon, gently fold the cream into the raspberry purée. Pour into a shallow pan and freeze. Stir occasionally until half-frozen and thick, then beat well with a fork.

Spoon a layer of ice cream into a large bar pan. Spoon the raspberry mixture randomly over the top. Using a sharp knife or skewer, swirl the mixture together. Freeze overnight.

Serve scoops of ice cream sprinkled with extra raspberries. Alternatively, remove the ice cream from the pan by briefly dipping the base in hot water. Invert onto a serving dish, cut into slices, and serve with raspberries.

Serves 8–10

Aloha, dude! When the surf's a wipeout and you're too hot to hula, here's a super-cool diversion to help chill you out.

hawaiian sundae

pineapple salsa
1 small pineapple, peeled, cored, and diced
1 tablespoon superfine sugar
1 small handful mint, chopped
1 tablespoon lime juice

mango sauce
2 large mangoes, peeled and chopped
1–2 tablespoons confectioners' sugar, sifted

1/4 cup unsalted macadamia nuts
1 quantity coconut lime ice cream (see page 349) or 4 cups other
    tropical-flavored ice cream

To make the pineapple salsa, put the diced pineapple in a plastic container
with a lid and add the sugar, mint, and lime juice. Seal the container and

shake vigorously to mix together well and crush the pineapple a bit. Refrigerate until needed.

To make the mango sauce, purée the mango flesh in a food processor, then push through a sieve. Whisk in enough confectioners' sugar to sweeten the mixture.

Dry-fry the macadamia nuts in a frying pan over high heat for about 2 minutes, tossing the pan regularly until the nuts are golden. Remove the nuts from the pan and set aside to cool. Roughly chop.

To assemble the sundaes, put two scoops of the ice cream in each of six sundae glasses. Add a spoonful of mango sauce and a large spoonful of the pineapple salsa. Top with the chopped nuts and serve immediately, drizzled with any remaining mango sauce.

Serves 6

hawaiian sundae

chocolate chestnut log

2/3 cup unsalted butter

1/3 cup superfine sugar

1 cup canned chestnut purée

1 1/4 cups chopped dark
   chocolate, melted

1/4 cup espresso coffee

1/4 cup brandy

3/4 cup unblanched almonds

1/2 cup superfine sugar, extra

Beat the butter and sugar until light and creamy. Mix in the chestnut purée, cooled melted chocolate, coffee, and brandy. Stir until smooth. Spoon into a bar pan lined with plastic wrap, then freeze overnight.

Put the almonds and extra sugar in a heavy-based frying pan over low heat—tilt the pan from side to side but don't stir. The sugar will form lumps, then melt into a caramel (take care it doesn't burn). Pour onto a cookie sheet lined with baking paper to set, then finely crush.

Cut the frozen chocolate mixture in half lengthwise, then wrap each half tightly in plastic wrap and roll into logs. Freeze for 30 minutes, then unwrap and roll in the crushed praline to coat. Slice and serve.

Serves 10–12

baked alaska

10 ounces (1 large) jelly roll
6 slices canned pineapple,
    juice reserved
6 scoops strawberry ice cream
    (see page 29) or store-bought

4 egg whites
$2/3$ cup superfine sugar

Preheat the oven to 450°F. Cut the jelly roll into six $1/2$-inch slices. Put them on a cookie sheet and brush lightly with the reserved pineapple juice. Top each with a slice of pineapple and a scoop of ice cream, then freeze while making the meringue.

Put the egg whites in a clean, dry bowl and whisk until soft peaks form. Gradually add the sugar, beating until glossy and stiff. Spread the meringue roughly over the ice cream and bake for 2–3 minutes or until light golden brown. Serve immediately.

Serves 6

cappuccino ice cream cakes

chocolate cake

3/4 cup unsalted butter

11/2 cups superfine sugar

21/2 teaspoons vanilla extract

3 eggs

1/2 cup self-rising flour

13/4 cups all-purpose flour

11/2 teaspoons baking soda

3/4 cup unsweetened cocoa
  powder

scant 11/4 cups buttermilk

1 tablespoon instant coffee
  granules

1 quantity vanilla ice cream
  (see page 16) or 4 cups
  store-bought, softened

1 cup heavy cream

1 tablespoon confectioners'
  sugar

3/4 heaped cup good-quality
  dark chocolate, melted

unsweetened cocoa powder,
  for dusting

Preheat the oven to 350°F. Lightly grease an 8-hole muffin pan.

To make the chocolate cake, beat the butter and sugar with electric beaters until light and creamy. Beat in the vanilla. Add the eggs, one at a time, beating well after each addition. Using a metal spoon, fold in the combined sifted flours, baking soda, and cocoa powder alternately with the buttermilk. Stir until just combined. Spoon the mixture into the muffin holes and bake for 25 minutes or until a skewer comes out clean. Cool in the pan briefly before turning onto a wire cake rack to cool.

Dissolve the coffee granules in 2 tablespoons of boiling water and allow to cool. Roughly break up the ice cream in a large bowl and stir until smooth. Stir in the coffee mixture and freeze until required.

Beat the cream and confectioners' sugar in a small bowl until soft peaks form. Chill in the refrigerator until needed.

Draw the outline of a small spoon eight times on a piece of baking paper, then turn the paper over. Spoon the melted chocolate into a paper piping bag or a clean plastic bag. Snip the end off the bag and draw a chocolate outline around the spoons, then fill in with melted chocolate. Allow the chocolate to set.

Cut the top off each cake. Use a spoon to scoop out some of the cake, leaving a $1/2$-inch shell (the leftover cake can be frozen for another use).

Soften the coffee ice cream with a spoon and pile it into the cakes so it comes slightly above the top. Add a dollop of cream mixture to represent cappuccino froth. Dust the tops with cocoa powder and serve with a chocolate spoon tucked into the cream.

Serves 8

cappuccino ice cream cakes

mexican chocolate, chili, and cinnamon ice cream

1^1/$_2$ cups milk
2 cups light whipping cream
4 small dried red chilies
3 cinnamon sticks

8 egg yolks
^{3}/$_4$ cup superfine sugar
1^1/$_4$ cups good-quality dark
    chocolate, grated

Put the milk, cream, chilies, and cinnamon sticks in a saucepan over medium heat. Stirring constantly, cook for a few minutes or until the sugar dissolves and the mixture is just about to boil. Remove from the heat and allow to infuse for 15 minutes. Reheat gently.

Beat the egg yolks and sugar in a large bowl. Whisk in ^{1}/$_4$ cup of the hot milk mixture. Whisk in the remaining milk mixture, then return to a clean saucepan and stir constantly over low–medium heat for 8–10 minutes or until the mixture thickens and coats the back of a spoon. Do not allow to boil. Remove from the heat, discard the chilies and cinnamon, and stir in the chocolate until melted and smooth. Cool slightly, then cover and refrigerate until cold.

Transfer to an ice cream maker and freeze according to manufacturer's instructions. Alternatively, transfer to a shallow metal tray and freeze, whisking every few hours until the texture is frozen and creamy. Freeze for 5 hours or overnight.

Makes 4 cups

warm caramel, nut, and banana parfait

1/3 cup butter
1/2 cup soft brown sugar
2 tablespoons maple syrup
1/4 cup sour cream
1 cup light whipping cream
1/2 cup condensed milk

2 bananas, sliced
12 scoops vanilla ice cream (see
  page 16) or store-bought
1/2 cup pecans, crushed

Put the butter, sugar, maple syrup, sour cream, and cream in a saucepan over medium heat. Stirring constantly, cook for a few minutes or until the sugar dissolves and the cream is just about to boil. Remove from the heat. When the bubbles have subsided, stir in the condensed milk, then leave to cool slightly.

To serve, layer the banana, ice cream, pecans, and warm caramel sauce in six sundae glasses.

Serves 6

hazelnut heaven ice cream sundae

choc-hazelnut shards
1/4 cup hazelnuts, roasted,
    skinned, and finely chopped
1/4 cup good-quality dark
    chocolate

choc-hazelnut cream
1/2 cup chocolate hazelnut
    spread
1/2 cup light whipping cream

Frangelico sauce
1/2 cup soft brown sugar
2 tablespoons light corn syrup
3 1/2 tablespoons unsalted
    butter, chopped

2 1/2 tablespoons Frangelico
    liqueur
1/4 cup light whipping cream

2 scoops chocolate ice cream
    (see page 28) or store-bought
2 scoops caramel ice cream
    (see page 18) or store-bought
2 scoops vanilla ice cream
    (see page 16) or store-bought
1/2 cup chocolate-coated malt
    balls
chopped hazelnuts, for sprinkling

Line a cookie sheet with baking paper. To make the choc-hazelnut shards, put the chocolate in a heatproof bowl. Fill a saucepan one-third full of water and bring to a simmer over medium heat. Set the bowl on top of the saucepan, making sure the base of the bowl does not touch the water. Stir occasionally until the chocolate has almost melted, then remove from the heat and stir until completely smooth. Spread very thinly over the baking paper. Sprinkle the hazelnuts over, then refrigerate for 6 hours or until hard. Using your hands, break the chocolate into large, irregular pieces, then store in an airtight container in the refrigerator for up to 5 days.

To make the choc-hazelnut cream, stir the chocolate hazelnut spread in a large bowl until smooth. Very lightly whip the cream and gently stir a third into the hazelnut spread. Stir in the remaining cream until combined and glossy. Chill until needed (this can be made up to 4 hours ahead).

To make the Frangelico sauce, put the sugar, corn syrup, and butter in a saucepan with 2 tablespoons of water and slowly bring to a boil. Cook over medium–high heat for 5 minutes or until smooth and thickened slightly. Remove from the heat and stir in the liqueur and cream. Use slightly warm or at room temperature (it will keep in an airtight container in the refrigerator for up to 5 days).

Arrange all the ice cream in a large serving dish. Pour over the Frangelico sauce, sprinkle with chocolate-coated malt balls, dollop with choc-hazelnut cream, pierce with choc-hazelnut shards, and sprinkle with chopped hazelnuts.

Serves 2

hazelnut heaven ice cream sundae

mocha custard sundae

3 teaspoons custard powder
2 tablespoons sugar
1 cup milk
1 cup light whipping cream
1/3 cup roasted coffee beans
1/2 cup dark chocolate, grated
2 tablespoons Irish cream liqueur,
   plus extra for drizzling
ready-made rich chocolate cake,
   cut into cubes, to serve
12 scoops vanilla ice cream
   (see page 16) or store-bought
chocolate-covered coffee beans,
   to serve

Put the custard powder and sugar in a saucepan. Whisk in the milk, cream, and coffee beans. Stir constantly over low–medium heat for 8–10 minutes or until the mixture thickens and coats the back of a spoon. Cover with plastic wrap and set aside to infuse for at least 10 minutes. Strain through a fine sieve into a clean pan and discard the coffee beans.

Gently reheat the custard, remove from the heat, and stir in the chocolate and liqueur until completely smooth. Allow to cool.

Put cubes of the cake in six sundae glasses and drizzle with a little extra liqueur. Top with scoops of vanilla ice cream and the mocha custard. Serve with chocolate-covered coffee beans.

Serves 6

caramel popcorn sundae

caramel sauce
1/3 cup superfine sugar
1/3 cup light whipping cream
1/2 teaspoon vanilla extract

2/3 cup light whipping cream
1 cup caramel or toffee-coated
   popcorn

1/4 cup roasted peanuts, chopped
1/4 cup roasted pecans, chopped
12 scoops vanilla ice cream (see
   page 16) or store-bought
2 bananas or 3 firm fresh figs,
   sliced (optional)

To make the caramel sauce, put the sugar and 1/3 cup water in a small saucepan and stir over medium heat until the sugar dissolves. Bring to a boil and cook, without stirring, for 8–10 minutes or until the sugar is dark golden and smells like toffee. Remove from the heat and carefully pour in the cream (it will splatter!), stirring constantly until smooth. Stir in the vanilla extract and set aside.

Whip the cream to firm peaks and chill. Combine the popcorn, peanuts, and pecans. Put two scoops of ice cream into each of six wide, flat sundae dishes. Add the sliced fruit, if using, and generously drizzle with the caramel sauce. Pipe the cream in swirls over the top, then sprinkle with the popcorn mixture. Serve immediately.

Serves 6

street vendor stand Arresting Asian flavors such as cardamom, star anise, ginger, chili, lemongrass, and even wasabi make for intriguing and tantalizing ices. Throw in some coconut milk,

sugar, and abundant tropical fruits like mangoes, dates, and lychees and, before you know it, you'll have an exotic experience happening right under your nose in your ice cream bowl!

black sesame seed ice cream

The people of many countries, especially those blessed with temperate climates, enjoy frozen ices in some form or another. These treats often become a culinary highlight of an international holiday— what could be more perfectly appropriate, for example, than eating green tea ice cream in Kyoto, savoring softly spiced kulfi on the streets of old Delhi, or sharing a serving of that most eccentric but delicious of frozen preparations, halo halo, while ambling along a pristine beach in the Philippines? Although some of these desserts and sweet snacks translate seamlessly to conditions in the kitchen back home, others—such as that extraordinary, stretchy treat from Turkey, sahlab ice cream—rely for utter authenticity on local ingredients that are simply unavailable outside their country of origin. What is eminently possible, however, is to take the flavor memories of, say, a Balinese honeymoon, a North African desert safari, or a tour through Mexico and apply them to basic iced dessert formulas. Thus, a peach and rosewater sorbet, saffron and raisin ice cream, scoops of palest green avocado ice cream, or a chili, lime, and lemongrass sorbet, will transport you back to far-flung places in no time at all. Conjure the sweet tastes of China, Korea, or Japan with ice creams infused with the sweet, nutty notes of black sesame seeds or red adzuki beans. Cardamom–coffee and sesame–halva flavored ices are superb dessert options for a Syrian or Lebanese-themed dinner party, while mango and star anise sorbet hints at the tropical wonders of Malaysia and Thailand. And so it goes . . .

323

deep-fried ice cream

2 quantities of vanilla ice cream
   (see page 16) or 8 cups
   store-bought
1 egg

1 cup all-purpose flour
1^1/$_2$ cups fine dry bread crumbs
2 tablespoons dried coconut
oil, for deep-frying

Make six large scoops of ice cream, about 3^1/$_4$ inches in diameter, and return them to the freezer.

In a bowl, whisk together the egg, flour, and ^{3}/$_4$ cup water to make a thick batter. Coat the ice cream balls with the batter, then roll in the combined bread crumbs and coconut to coat thickly. Freeze for 48 hours.

Heat the oil in a deep fryer or large heavy-based saucepan to 375°F or until a cube of bread dropped in the oil turns golden brown in 10 seconds. Slide in one ice cream ball at a time and cook for a few seconds, until golden—take care not to melt the ice cream. Serve at once.

Serves 6

papaya lime sorbet

1 cup superfine sugar
2 small ripe papaya, peeled
    and chopped
1$^1/_2$ tablespoons fresh lime juice

Put the sugar and $^1/_3$ cup water in a small saucepan over medium heat. Stirring constantly, cook for a few minutes or until the sugar dissolves. Bring to a boil, then remove from the heat and allow to cool completely.

Put the papaya in a food processor and blend until smooth. Blend in the cooled sugar syrup, then the lime juice.

Transfer to an ice cream maker and freeze according to manufacturer's instructions. Alternatively, transfer to a shallow metal tray and freeze, whisking every couple of hours until frozen and smooth. Freeze for 4 hours or overnight. Store in the freezer until ready to serve.

Makes 4 cups

Redolent of mysterious spices, kulfi is the subcontinent's
dense, perfumed, and lovely gift to the ice cream world.

kulfi

1/4 cup shelled pistachio nuts
6 cups milk
21 cardamom pods
1/2 cup superfine sugar
1/2 teaspoon finely grated lime zest

Preheat the broiler to medium. Spread the pistachios on a cookie sheet
and broil for 3 minutes or until aromatic and lightly toasted. Set aside to
cool slightly, then roughly chop.

Put the milk and nine cardamom pods in a large heavy-based saucepan.
Stirring constantly, cook for a few minutes, until the milk is just about to
boil. Reduce the heat and simmer for 15–20 minutes or until the liquid
has reduced by one-third.

Strain the hot milk into a freezerproof container. Add the sugar and stir until it has dissolved. Stir in half the pistachios and all the lime zest, then set aside to cool for 30 minutes. Transfer the remaining pistachios to an airtight container.

Freeze the infused milk until almost firm, stirring every 30 minutes—this can take 3–6 hours, depending on the temperature of your freezer.

Rinse eight $^2/_3$-cup molds with cold water, shaking out the excess. Pack the kulfi into the molds and freeze until completely firm.

Remove the molds from the freezer 5 minutes before serving. Turn the kulfi out onto serving plates and sprinkle with the reserved pistachios. Lightly crush the remaining cardamom pods to release some of the seeds. Sprinkle a few seeds over the kulfi and sprinkle the pods around the base.

Serves 8

kulfi

chili, lime, and lemongrass sorbet

2 cups lime juice, freshly
   squeezed and strained
1 teaspoon lime zest, grated
1$2/3$ cups superfine sugar
4–6 Kaffir lime leaves

3 lemongrass stems, white part
   only, finely chopped
3 small red chilies, halved and
   seeds removed

Put the lime juice, lime zest, sugar, and 1$1/2$ cups water in a saucepan and stir over medium heat until the sugar has dissolved.

Add the lime leaves, lemongrass, and chilies and bring to a boil. Reduce the heat and simmer for 5 minutes, then remove from the heat and allow to cool to room temperature for the flavors to infuse. Strain into a bowl, cover, and refrigerate until cold.

Transfer to an ice cream maker and freeze according to manufacturer's instructions. Alternatively, transfer to a shallow metal tray and freeze, whisking every couple of hours until frozen and smooth. Freeze for 4 hours or overnight. Store in the freezer until ready to serve.

Makes 4 cups

avocado ice cream

1 large ripe avocado	1 teaspoon vanilla extract
1¹/₂ cups light whipping cream	1 large ripe banana
¹/₄ cup honey	2 egg whites, stiffly beaten

Blend the avocado, cream, honey, vanilla extract, and banana in small batches in a blender until thick. Pour into a bowl, then carefully fold in the egg whites using a metal spoon.

Transfer to an ice cream maker and freeze according to manufacturer's instructions. Alternatively, transfer to a shallow metal tray and freeze, whisking every couple of hours until frozen and creamy. Freeze for 5 hours or overnight. Soften in the fridge for 30 minutes before serving.

Makes 4 cups

With their cheery pink tones and unbelievably fragrant flesh,

guavas were destined to star in a sorbet.

guava sorbet

three 14^1/$_2$-ounce cans guava in syrup
^{1}/$_3$ cup superfine sugar
1 cup orange juice, freshly squeezed and strained

Strain the guava, catching the syrup in a bowl. Scoop the seeds from the guava into a sieve over the same bowl to collect any juices. Using the back of a spoon, press down on the seeds several times to extract any remaining juice. Discard the seeds.

Put the sugar and ^{3}/$_4$ cup water in a small saucepan over medium heat. Stirring constantly, cook for a few minutes, until the sugar has dissolved. Bring to a boil. Add the guava syrup and guava pieces and simmer for 5 minutes. Stir in the orange juice, then set aside to cool completely and allow the flavors to develop.

Scoop the guava out of the syrup using a slotted spoon (reserve the syrup). Put in a food processor and purée until smooth. Push the purée through a sieve back into the syrup and mix well.

Transfer to an ice cream maker and freeze according to manufacturer's instructions. Alternatively, transfer to a shallow metal tray and freeze, whisking every couple of hours until the sorbet is frozen and smooth. Freeze for 4 hours or overnight. Store in the freezer until ready to serve.

Makes 4 cups

guava sorbet

moroccan mint tea sorbet

3 teaspoons Chinese gunpowder
   tea (green tea)
2 large handfuls spearmint, torn
1 teaspoon lemon juice
3/4 cup superfine sugar

2 egg whites
small handful finely chopped
   spearmint leaves, extra
   to serve

Bring 3 1/2 cups water to a boil in a saucepan. Add the green tea, torn spearmint leaves, lemon juice, and sugar. Stirring constantly, cook for a few minutes, until the sugar has dissolved. Remove from the heat and allow to steep for 5 minutes. Pour through a muslin-lined sieve into a bowl and allow to cool. Add the egg whites and whisk to combine. Cover and refrigerate until cold.

Transfer to an ice cream maker and freeze according to manufacturer's instructions, adding the finely chopped spearmint halfway through. Alternatively, transfer to a shallow metal tray and freeze, whisking every couple of hours until frozen and smooth, adding the spearmint during the final beating. Freeze for 4 hours or overnight. Store in the freezer until ready to serve.

Makes 4 cups

persian nougat ice cream

1/3 cup blanched almonds, roasted	6 egg yolks
1/3 cup pistachios	1/3 cup superfine sugar, extra
1/2 cup superfine sugar	1/3 cup orange liqueur
	2 cups light whipping cream

Sprinkle all the nuts on a greased cookie sheet. Put the sugar and 1/4 cup water in a saucepan and stir over low heat until the sugar has dissolved. Increase the heat, bring to a boil, and cook for 6 minutes or until dark golden. Pour over the nuts. Allow to cool and harden, then crush.

Whisk the egg yolks and extra sugar in a large bowl. Whisk in the liqueur. Transfer to a saucepan and stir constantly over low–medium heat for 8–10 minutes or until thick and foamy. Remove from the heat, cover, and leave to cool. Whip the cream to soft peaks and gently fold into the custard.

Transfer to an ice cream maker and freeze according to manufacturer's instructions, adding the crushed nuts halfway through. Alternatively, transfer to a shallow metal tray and freeze, whisking every couple of hours until frozen and creamy, adding the nuts during the final beating. Freeze for 5 hours or overnight. Soften in the fridge for 30 minutes before serving.

Makes 4 cups

No machine needed for this scrumptious parfait, featuring dried figs doused into life with sticky almond liqueur.

dried fig and almond parfait

2 cups soft dried figs
$1/4$ cup Amaretto
7 large egg yolks
2 tablespoons soft brown sugar
1 tablespoon honey

$1/2$ teaspoon vanilla extract
$2/3$ cup almonds, lightly toasted
$1 1/4$ cups heavy whipping cream

Cut the figs into quarters and put them in a small saucepan with the liqueur. Stir occasionally over low heat for about 5 minutes or until the figs absorb all the liqueur and become soft. Remove from the heat and leave to cool.

Put the egg yolks, sugar, honey, and vanilla extract in a food processor and blend on high, scraping down the sides occasionally until the mixture is thick, pale, and creamy. This will take about 5 minutes. Add the figs and pulse a few times—the mixture should still be chunky. Transfer to a bowl and fold in the almonds.

Pour the cream into a chilled bowl and whip to soft peaks. Fold a third of the cream into the fig mixture, then fold in the remainder.

Line a large bar pan with plastic wrap (if you wipe it first with a clean, damp sponge, the plastic will stick to the side and make it easier to fill). Smooth the parfait mixture into the pan, fold the plastic wrap over to cover the parfait, then freeze. The parfait will be set in 4 hours, but the flavors will develop further if left overnight or longer.

To serve, use the plastic wrap to help pull the parfait out of the pan. Invert onto a chilled serving platter and remove the wrap. Cut the parfait into slices and serve.

Serves 8–10

dried fig and almond parfait

jasmine snow

3/4 cup confectioners' sugar
2 teaspoons mint, chopped
2 cups hot, weak jasmine tea
1 tablespoon lemon juice

2 tablespoons orange juice
1 egg white, beaten
orange zest strips, to garnish

Put the confectioners' sugar and mint in a bowl. Strain the hot tea into the bowl and stir until the sugar dissolves. Stir in the lemon and orange juices, then allow to cool.

Transfer to an ice cream maker and freeze according to manufacturer's instructions, adding the beaten egg white halfway through. Alternatively, transfer to a shallow metal tray and freeze, whisking every couple of hours until frozen and smooth, adding the egg white during the final beating. Freeze for 4 hours or overnight. Store in the freezer until ready to serve.

To serve, scrape the sorbet into a serving dish to resemble large snowflakes.

Makes 4 cups

japanese red bean ice cream

1 cup milk
1 cup light whipping cream
1/2 cup superfine sugar
1/2 teaspoon vanilla extract

4 egg yolks
1 1/2 cups sweet adzuki bean
    paste (anko)

Put the milk, cream, sugar, and vanilla extract in a saucepan over medium heat. Stirring constantly, cook for a few minutes or until the sugar dissolves and the milk is just about to boil. Remove from the heat.

Whisk the egg yolks in a large bowl. Whisk in 1/4 cup of the hot milk until smooth. Whisk in the remaining milk, then return to a clean saucepan and stir constantly over low–medium heat for 8–10 minutes or until the mixture thickens and coats the back of a spoon. Do not allow to boil. Add half the adzuki bean paste to the warm custard, stirring vigorously to combine. Cool slightly, then refrigerate until cold.

Transfer to an ice cream maker and freeze according to manufacturer's instructions, adding the remaining bean paste halfway through. Alternatively, transfer to a shallow metal tray and freeze, whisking every few hours until frozen and creamy, adding the bean paste during the final beating.

Makes 4 cups

Nutrient-rich, super-ripe bananas and gooey fresh dates make this ice cream a tonic for the body as well as the soul.

coconut, banana, and date ice cream

1^1/$_2$ cups coconut cream
1^1/$_2$ cups coconut milk
^{2}/$_3$ cup superfine sugar
6 egg yolks
2 ripe bananas, mashed
^{3}/$_4$ heaped cup fresh dates, pitted and finely chopped

Put the coconut cream, coconut milk, and sugar in a saucepan over medium heat. Stirring constantly, cook for a few minutes or until the sugar dissolves and the milk is just about to boil. Remove from the heat.

Whisk the egg yolks in a large bowl until well combined. Whisk in ^{1}/$_4$ cup of the hot coconut cream mixture until smooth. Whisk in the remaining coconut cream mixture, then return to a clean saucepan and stir constantly over low–medium heat for 8–10 minutes or until the mixture thickens and coats the back of a spoon. Do not allow to boil. Set aside to cool slightly, then refrigerate until cold.

Stir the mashed bananas into the cold custard. Transfer to an ice cream maker and freeze according to manufacturer's instructions, adding the chopped dates near the end of the churning process. Alternatively, transfer to a shallow metal tray and freeze, whisking every couple of hours until frozen and creamy, adding the dates during the final beating. Freeze overnight. Soften in the fridge for 30 minutes before serving.

Serving suggestion: If you have any caramel sauce left over from another recipe, try drizzling it over this ice cream.

Makes 4 cups

coconut, banana, and date ice cream

nashi pear and sake sorbet

1¹/2 cups superfine sugar
3 Nashi pears, peeled and
   chopped
¹/2 teaspoon fresh ginger, finely
   grated

2 tablespoons lemon juice
1¹/2 cups good-quality sake, plus
   extra to serve

Put the sugar and 1¹/2 cups water in a saucepan over high heat and stir until the sugar has dissolved. Bring to a boil, add the pear and ginger, and bring to a boil again. Reduce the heat and simmer for 15–20 minutes or until the pear is very soft. Remove from the heat and allow to cool.

Purée the pear mixture and lemon juice in a food processor until very smooth. Push the mixture through a fine sieve, then stir in the sake.

Transfer to an ice cream maker and freeze according to manufacturer's instructions. Alternatively, transfer to a shallow metal tray and freeze, whisking every couple of hours until frozen and smooth. Freeze for 4 hours or overnight. Soften the sorbet in the fridge for 15–20 minutes before serving with a dash of sake.

Makes 4 cups

coconut lime ice cream

1/4 cup dried coconut
1 1/2 tablespoons lime zest,
   grated
1/3 cup lime juice
1/3 cup coconut milk powder

1 quantity vanilla ice cream
   (see page 16) or 4 cups
   store-bought, softened
coconut macaroon biscuits,
   to serve (optional)

Put the coconut, lime zest, lime juice, and coconut milk powder in a bowl. Mix together well.

Fold the coconut mixture through the ice cream using a large metal spoon, working quickly so the ice cream doesn't melt. Freeze until firm.

349

To serve, put three scoops into each of four short glasses, perhaps with some coconut macaroon biscuits on the side.

Makes 4 cups

Ever wondered how tropical types sustain themselves through long, steamy, sticky-hot days? Here's your answer: halo halo.

halo halo

3/4 cup dried chickpeas

3/4 cup dried red kidney beans

one 3-ounce packet of fruit-flavored gelatin

1/2 cup superfine sugar

2 lemongrass stems, bruised

2 tablespoons fresh ginger, sliced

2/3 cup canned jackfruit, drained and cut into 3/4-inch squares

18 canned whole lychees, halved (reserve the syrup)

1/4 cup canned coconut flesh, drained and shredded (optional)

1 mango, cut into 1/2-inch cubes

3 cups shaved ice

1 1/2 cups coconut milk

3 teaspoons lime juice

2 tablespoons superfine sugar, extra

1/3 quantity vanilla ice cream (see page 16) or 1 1/3 cups store-bought

Put the chickpeas and red kidney beans in separate bowls. Cover with plenty of water and soak overnight.

Make the gelatin according to the packet instructions, using only half the quantity of water prescribed. Set in a bar pan until very firm. When the jelly has set, cut it into 3/4-inch cubes.

Drain the chickpeas and kidney beans. Put them in separate saucepans with plenty of water. Add 1/4 cup of sugar, a lemongrass stem, and half the sliced ginger to each saucepan. Bring to a simmer and cook until tender (about 30 minutes for the beans and 50 minutes for the chickpeas). Drain and discard the lemongrass and ginger, then mix the beans and chickpeas together in a bowl. Allow to cool.

Put the jackfruit, lychees, 1/2 cup of the reserved lychee syrup, coconut meat, and mango in a bowl. Gently mix together, then divide among six sundae glasses. Top each with 2 tablespoons of the chickpea and kidney bean mixture. Add the gelatin cubes and shaved ice.

Combine the coconut milk, lime juice, and extra sugar and stir until the sugar has dissolved. Pour over the shaved ice, top with a scoop of ice cream, and serve immediately.

Serves 6

halo halo

chinese ginger and roasted almond ice cream

1/2 cup milk
1 1/2 cups light whipping cream
2/3 cup superfine sugar
6 egg yolks

1/4 cup glacé ginger, very finely
    chopped
1/3 cup whole blanched almonds,
    toasted and chopped
glacé ginger, extra to serve

Put the milk, cream, and sugar in a saucepan over medium heat. Stirring constantly, cook for a few minutes or until the sugar dissolves and the mixture is just about to boil. Remove from the heat.

Whisk the egg yolks in a large bowl. Whisk in 1/4 cup of the hot milk until smooth. Whisk in the remaining milk, then return to a clean saucepan and stir constantly over low–medium heat for 8–10 minutes or until the mixture thickens and coats the back of a spoon. Do not allow to boil. Stir in the glacé ginger, cool slightly, then cover and refrigerate until cold.

Transfer to an ice cream maker and freeze according to manufacturer's instructions, adding the almonds halfway through. Alternatively, transfer to a shallow metal tray and freeze, whisking every couple of hours until frozen and creamy, adding the almonds during the final beating. Freeze for 5 hours or overnight. Serve sprinkled with extra glacé ginger.

Makes 4 cups

wasabi ice cream

1¹/₂ cups milk
1¹/₂ cups light whipping cream
²/₃ cup superfine sugar

8 egg yolks
1 tablespoon wasabi paste

Put the milk, cream, and sugar in a saucepan over medium heat. Stirring constantly, cook for a few minutes or until the sugar dissolves and the milk is just about to boil. Remove from the heat.

Whisk the egg yolks in a large bowl. Stir in the wasabi paste. Whisk in ¹/₄ cup of the hot milk mixture until smooth. Whisk in the remaining milk mixture, then return to a clean saucepan and stir constantly over low–medium heat for 8–10 minutes or until the mixture thickens and coats the back of a spoon. Do not allow to boil. Allow to cool slightly, then refrigerate until cold.

Transfer to an ice cream maker and freeze according to manufacturer's instructions. Alternatively, transfer to a shallow metal tray and freeze, whisking every couple of hours until frozen and creamy. Freeze for 5 hours or overnight. Soften in the fridge for 30 minutes before serving.

Makes 4 cups

green tea ice cream

1 cup milk
2 1/2 cups light whipping cream
1 vanilla bean, split lengthwise
    and seeds scraped
9 egg yolks
2/3 cup superfine sugar
3 teaspoons matcha (green tea
    powder)

Banana tempura (optional)
oil, for deep-frying
1 egg
2/3 cup tempura flour
4 small bananas, cut in half
    lengthwise, then cut in
    half crossways
superfine sugar, for sprinkling
warmed honey, to serve
    (optional)

Put the milk, cream, vanilla bean, and vanilla seeds in a saucepan over medium heat. Stirring constantly, cook for a few minutes or until the sugar dissolves and the mixture is just about to boil. Remove from the heat and allow to infuse for 15 minutes. Discard the vanilla bean and gently reheat.

Beat the egg yolks and sugar in a large bowl until creamy. Whisk in 1/4 cup of the hot milk mixture until smooth. Whisk in the remaining milk mixture, then return to a clean saucepan and stir constantly over low–medium heat for 8–10 minutes or until the mixture thickens and coats the back of a spoon. Do not allow to boil. Stir in the green tea powder, cool slightly, then refrigerate until cold.

Transfer to an ice cream maker and freeze according to manufacturer's instructions. Alternatively, transfer to a shallow metal tray and freeze, whisking every couple of hours until frozen and creamy. Freeze for 5 hours or overnight. Soften in the fridge for 30 minutes before serving.

If making the banana tempura, heat the oil in a deep fryer or heavy-based saucepan to 325°F or until a cube of bread dropped in the oil browns in 20 seconds. Quickly mix together the egg and 3/4 cup iced water in a bowl, then mix in the tempura flour with a fork. Do not whisk the batter—it must be lumpy.

Dip the banana pieces in the batter and deep-fry a few at a time for 2 minutes or until crisp and golden. Sprinkle with sugar and serve four pieces of banana with a scoop of ice cream, drizzled with warmed honey.

Makes 4 cups ice cream
Serves 4 with the banana tempura

green tea ice cream

cardamom coffee ice cream

6 cardamom pods, lightly
  crushed
1 1/2 cups milk
1 cup heavy cream

1/2 cup superfine sugar
1 tablespoon instant coffee
  granules
5 egg yolks

Put the cardamom pods in a saucepan with the milk, cream, sugar, and coffee over medium heat. Stirring constantly, cook for a few minutes or until the sugar dissolves and the milk is just about to boil. Set aside and leave to infuse for 20 minutes. Discard the pods and gently reheat.

Whisk the egg yolks in a large bowl. Whisk in 1/4 cup of the hot milk mixture until smooth. Whisk in the remaining milk mixture, then return to a clean saucepan and stir constantly over low–medium heat for 8–10 minutes or until the mixture thickens and coats the back of a spoon. Do not allow to boil. Cool slightly, then cover and refrigerate until cold.

Transfer to an ice cream maker and freeze according to manufacturer's instructions. Alternatively, transfer to a shallow metal tray and freeze, whisking every couple of hours until frozen and creamy. Freeze for 5 hours or overnight. Soften in the fridge for 30 minutes before serving.

Makes 4 cups

frozen yogurt ambrosia

2/3 cup light whipping cream
1/2 cup superfine sugar
1 teaspoon vanilla extract
1 1/2 teaspoons orange blossom
   or rose water
1 cup plain yogurt

topping
3 tablespoons sunflower seeds,
   toasted
3 tablespoons hazelnuts, chopped
3 tablespoons walnuts, chopped
1 tablespoon dried coconut
1/3 cup dried apricots, chopped
1/3 cup soft dried figs, chopped

Whip the cream until just thick, then fold in the sugar, vanilla extract, orange blossom water, and yogurt.

Transfer to an ice cream maker and freeze according to manufacturer's instructions. Alternatively, transfer to a shallow metal tray and freeze, whisking every couple of hours until frozen and creamy. Freeze for 5 hours or overnight. Soften in the fridge for 30 minutes before serving.

Mix all the topping ingredients together. Scoop the frozen yogurt into sundae glasses, sprinkle with the topping, and serve.

Serves 4–6

Capture the elusive, delicate perfume of the elegant lychee and fine strawberries, too, in this plush, icy dessert.

lychee and strawberry ice cream

1²/₃ cups strawberries

³/₄ cup superfine sugar

2¹/₂ cups canned lychees
   in syrup

1¹/₂ cups milk

2 cups light whipping cream

6 egg yolks

Hull and roughly chop the strawberries. Place them in a bowl, along with any juices. Sprinkle with 1 tablespoon of the sugar and set aside for 30 minutes to steep.

Drain and finely chop the lychees, reserving ¹/₂ cup of the syrup.

Put the milk, cream, and remaining sugar in a saucepan over medium heat. Stirring constantly, cook for a few minutes or until the sugar dissolves and the mixture is just about to boil. Remove from the heat.

Whisk the egg yolks in a large bowl. Whisk in $^1/4$ cup of the hot milk mixture until smooth. Whisk in the remaining milk mixture, then return to a clean saucepan and stir constantly over low–medium heat for 8–10 minutes or until the mixture thickens and coats the back of a spoon. Do not allow to boil. Strain through a fine sieve and set aside to cool.

Gently stir the strawberries and strawberry juice, lychees, and lychee syrup into the custard. Transfer to an ice cream maker and freeze according to manufacturer's instructions. Alternatively, transfer to a shallow metal tray and freeze, whisking every couple of hours until frozen and creamy. Freeze for 5 hours or overnight.

Soften the ice cream in the fridge for 30 minutes before serving.

Makes 4 cups

lychee and strawberry ice cream

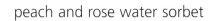

peach and rose water sorbet

1³/₄ cups peach-flavored tea
1¹/₃ cups superfine sugar
6 peaches
¹/₃ cup rose water

Pour half the peach tea into a small saucepan. Add the sugar and stir until the sugar has dissolved. Bring to a boil and cook for 2 minutes, then remove from the heat and set aside to cool.

Cut the peaches into quarters, removing the pits. Put the peaches and remaining peach tea in a saucepan and simmer for 10 minutes. Reserving the liquid, remove the peaches with a slotted spoon and peel off the skins. Set the peaches aside to cool.

Using a hand blender or small food processor, purée the peaches, poaching liquid, sugar syrup, and rose water until smooth. Transfer to an ice cream maker and freeze according to manufacturer's instructions. Alternatively, transfer to a shallow metal tray and freeze, whisking every couple of hours until frozen and smooth. Freeze for 4 hours or overnight. Store in the freezer until ready to serve.

Makes 4 cups

sahlab ice cream

1 1/4 cups light whipping cream
heaping 3/4 cup superfine sugar
2 1/2 cups milk
1/3 cup sahlab powder
2 1/2 teaspoons orange flower
  water

1/8 teaspoon (2 pebble-size
  pieces) mastic, crushed
chopped pistachios and ground
  cinnamon, to serve

Put the cream, sugar, and 1 3/4 cups milk in a saucepan. Bring to a simmer.

Combine the remaining milk and sahlab powder and mix until smooth. Add to the saucepan in a thin, steady stream, then stir constantly over low–medium heat for 8–10 minutes or until the mixture thickens and coats the back of a spoon. Do not allow to boil. Remove from the heat, add the orange flower water and mastic, and stir until the mastic dissolves. Set aside to cool slightly, then cover and refrigerate until cold.

Transfer to an ice cream maker and freeze according to manufacturer's instructions. Alternatively, transfer to a shallow metal tray and freeze, whisking every few hours until frozen and creamy. Freeze for 5 hours or overnight. Serve sprinkled with chopped pistachios and cinnamon.

Makes 4 cups

Lemon and orange have a delectable way of permeating frozen treats—and the poppy seed crunch is totally addictive.

citrus and poppy seed ice cream

2 cups light whipping cream
1 1/2 cups milk
1/2 cup superfine sugar
zest of 1 orange, cut into
    large strips
zest of 1/2 lemon, cut into
    large strips

1/2 teaspoon vanilla extract
4 large egg yolks
1/2 cup orange juice, freshly
    squeezed
zest of 1/2 orange, finely grated
zest of 1/4 lemon, finely grated
1/2 teaspoon poppy seeds

Put the cream, milk, sugar, orange zest, lemon zest, and vanilla in a saucepan over medium heat. Stirring constantly, cook for a few minutes or until the sugar dissolves and the mixture is just about to boil. Remove from the heat, cover, and set aside to infuse for 10 minutes. Pour through a sieve into a saucepan and gently reheat.

Whisk the egg yolks in a large bowl. Whisk in 1/4 cup of the hot cream mixture until smooth. Whisk in the remaining cream mixture, then return

to a clean saucepan and stir constantly over low–medium heat for 8–10 minutes or until the mixture thickens and coats the back of a spoon. Do not allow to boil. Remove from the heat and set aside to cool slightly, then stir in the orange juice and grated orange and lemon zest. Cover and refrigerate until cold.

Transfer to an ice cream maker and freeze according to manufacturer's instructions, adding the poppy seeds halfway through. Alternatively, transfer to a shallow metal tray and freeze, whisking every couple of hours until frozen and creamy, adding the poppy seeds during the final beating. Freeze for 5 hours or overnight.

Soften the ice cream in the fridge for 30 minutes before serving.

Makes 4 cups

citrus and poppy seed ice cream

watermelon and rose water ice

2 pound 4 ounce piece of
    watermelon, rind removed
2 teaspoons lime juice
1/4 cup superfine sugar

1/4 cup citrus-flavored vodka
2 teaspoons rose water

Coarsely chop the watermelon, removing the seeds—you should have about 2 1/2 cups of flesh. Put the watermelon in a food processor. Add the lime juice and sugar. Process until smooth, then strain through a fine sieve. Stir in the vodka and rose water, then taste—if the watermelon is not very sweet, you may have to add a little more sugar.

Pour the mixture into a shallow tray and freeze for 2 1/2 hours or until the mixture starts to freeze around the edges.

Scrape the frozen edges back into the mixture with a fork. Repeat every 30 minutes for 3 hours or until evenly sized ice crystals form. If you are preparing the ice ahead of time, store it in the freezer and scrape once again just before serving. To serve, scrape into dishes with a fork.

Serving suggestion: Serve a scoop in a shot glass with vodka.

Makes 4 cups

sesame halva ice cream

1¼ cups milk
1¼ cups light whipping cream
1 cup soft brown sugar
6 large egg yolks

¼ teaspoon vanilla extract
⅔ cup tahini
¼ cup sesame seeds, toasted
and lightly crushed

Put the milk, cream, and sugar in a saucepan over medium heat. Stirring constantly, cook for a few minutes or until the sugar dissolves and the milk is just about to boil. Remove from the heat.

Whisk the egg yolks in a large bowl. Whisk in ¼ cup of the hot milk mixture until smooth. Stir in the remaining milk, then return to a clean saucepan and stir constantly over low–medium heat for 8–10 minutes or until the mixture thickens and coats the back of a spoon. Do not allow to boil. Stir in the vanilla and tahini and set aside to cool, stirring as needed to break up the tahini. Strain, then cover and refrigerate until cold.

Stir in the sesame seeds, then transfer to an ice cream maker and freeze according to manufacturer's instructions. Alternatively, transfer to a shallow metal tray and freeze, whisking every couple of hours until frozen and creamy. Freeze for 5 hours or overnight.

Makes 4 cups

Tea, sugar, and spice are very, very nice . . . and bring an enticing new complexion to a simple confection.

chai ice cream

2 cups light whipping cream
1^1/$_2$ cups milk
^{1}/$_2$ cup superfine sugar
1 tablespoon black tea leaves
2 cinnamon sticks
8 whole cardamom pods
6 whole cloves

1^1/$_2$ tablespoons fresh ginger, sliced
^{1}/$_2$ teaspoon vanilla extract
1^1/$_4$-inch strip of orange zest
4 large egg yolks

Put the cream, milk, half the sugar, the tea leaves, cinnamon sticks, cardamom pods, cloves, ginger, vanilla extract, and orange zest in a saucepan over medium heat. Stirring constantly, cook for a few minutes or until the sugar dissolves and the mixture is just about to boil. Remove from the heat, then cover and set aside to infuse for 15 minutes. Pour through a muslin-lined fine sieve into a saucepan and gently reheat.

Whisk the egg yolks and remaining sugar in a large bowl until well combined. Whisk in $1/4$ cup of the hot cream mixture until smooth. Whisk in the remaining cream mixture, then return to a clean saucepan and stir constantly over low–medium heat for 8–10 minutes or until the mixture thickens and coats the back of a spoon. Do not allow to boil. Set aside to cool slightly and refrigerate until cold.

Transfer to an ice cream maker and freeze according to manufacturer's instructions. Alternatively, transfer to a shallow metal tray and freeze, whisking every couple of hours until the ice cream is frozen and creamy. Freeze for 5 hours or overnight.

Soften the ice cream in the fridge for 30 minutes before serving.

Makes 4 cups

chai ice cream

ginger and tofu ice cream

¼ cup fresh ginger, thinly sliced
1½ cups superfine sugar
4 tablespoons light corn syrup
two 10½-ounce packets
   silken tofu

1 egg white, lightly beaten
finely chopped glacé ginger,
   to serve (optional)

Put the ginger and 1½ cups water in a saucepan. Bring to a boil, reduce the heat, and simmer for 5 minutes. Add the sugar, stir until dissolved, then simmer for an additional 5 minutes. Blend the mixture until fine, then strain and stir in the light corn syrup. You should have about 1½ cups of syrup.

Drain the tofu well, then process until smooth. Stir in the ginger syrup.

Transfer to an ice cream maker and freeze according to manufacturer's instructions. Alternatively, transfer to a shallow metal tray and freeze, whisking every couple of hours until frozen and creamy. Freeze for 5 hours or overnight. Soften in the fridge for 30 minutes before serving.

Serve sprinkled with finely chopped glacé ginger if desired.

Makes 4 cups

kiwi fruit sorbet

6 large kiwi fruit, peeled
and chopped
$1/3$ cup sugar
2 egg whites

Put the kiwi fruit in a saucepan with the sugar and 1 cup water. Stirring constantly, cook for a few minutes or until the sugar has dissolved. Bring to a boil, then reduce the heat and simmer for 5 minutes or until the fruit is soft. Remove from the heat and cool slightly.

Purée the kiwi fruit mixture in a food processor in batches until smooth.

Whisk the egg whites to firm peaks, then fold into the kiwi fruit mixture. Transfer to an ice cream maker and freeze according to manufacturer's instructions. Alternatively, transfer to a shallow metal tray and freeze, whisking every couple of hours until frozen and smooth. Freeze for 4 hours or overnight. Store in the freezer until ready to serve.

Makes 4 cups

Passion fruits are such potent little things, and palatable, too—
see if you can resist them paired with heavenly pistachios.

passion fruit and pistachio ice cream

1/2 cup milk
1 1/2 cups light whipping cream
3/4 cup superfine sugar
6 egg yolks
pulp of 8 passion fruit

1/3 cup shelled pistachios,
   chopped
extra passion fruit pulp, to serve
   (optional)

Put the milk, cream, and sugar in a saucepan over medium heat. Stirring constantly, cook for a few minutes or until the sugar dissolves and the mixture is just about to boil. Remove from the heat.

Whisk the egg yolks in a large bowl until well combined. Whisk in 1/4 cup of the hot milk mixture until smooth. Whisk in the remaining milk mixture, then return to a clean saucepan and stir constantly over low–medium heat for 8–10 minutes or until the mixture thickens and coats the back of a spoon. Do not allow to boil. Set aside to cool slightly, then cover and refrigerate until cold.

Reserve 1/4 cup of the passion fruit pulp. Put the remainder in a small saucepan. Warm over medium heat for 1–2 minutes. Remove from the heat, strain, then set aside to cool. Fold the passion fruit juice and reserved passion fruit pulp through the custard mixture.

Transfer to an ice cream maker and freeze according to manufacturer's instructions, adding the pistachios halfway through. Alternatively, transfer to a shallow metal tray and freeze, whisking every couple of hours until frozen and creamy, adding the pistachios during the final beating. Freeze for 5 hours or overnight. Soften in the fridge for 30 minutes before serving.

Serve drizzled with extra passion fruit pulp if desired.

Makes 4 cups

passion fruit and pistachio ice cream

tamarillo ice cream

2 cups superfine sugar

8 tamarillos

3 cups light whipping cream

5 egg yolks

Put the sugar and 2 cups water in a saucepan over medium heat. Stirring constantly, cook until the sugar dissolves, then bring to a boil for 5 minutes. Add the tamarillos. Return to a boil, then reduce the heat and simmer for 4–6 minutes or until soft. Remove from the heat and cool to room temperature. Purée the tamarillos and syrup in a food processor until smooth. Sieve to remove the seeds.

Bring the cream just to a boil over medium heat. Whisk the egg yolks in a large bowl. Whisk in $1/4$ cup of the hot cream until smooth, then whisk in the remaining cream and return to a clean saucepan. Stir constantly over low–medium heat for 8–10 minutes or until the mixture thickens and coats the back of a spoon. Do not allow to boil. Stir in the tamarillo purée. Cool slightly, then refrigerate until chilled.

Transfer to an ice cream maker and freeze according to manufacturer's instructions. Alternatively, transfer to a shallow metal tray and freeze, whisking every couple of hours until frozen and creamy. Freeze for 5 hours or overnight. Soften in the fridge for 30 minutes before serving.

Makes 4 cups

saffron and raisin ice cream

1/2 cup raisins, chopped	2 wide lemon zest strips
large pinch of saffron threads	2 cinnamon sticks, broken in half
2/3 cup milk	2/3 cup superfine sugar
2 cups light whipping cream	6 large egg yolks

Put the raisins in a small bowl and add enough boiling water to just cover. Soak for 1 hour, then squeeze out the excess liquid. Sprinkle the saffron over 1 tablespoon of hot water in a small bowl and let sit for 1 hour.

Put the milk, cream, lemon zest, and cinnamon in a saucepan over medium heat. Stirring constantly, simmer for a few minutes, then set aside to infuse for 30 minutes. Strain, then add the saffron mixture.

Whisk the egg yolks in a large bowl. Whisk in 1/4 cup of the hot milk until smooth, then whisk in the remainder. Return to a clean saucepan and stir constantly over low–medium heat until the mixture thickens. Do not allow to boil. Cool slightly, add the raisins, then refrigerate until cold.

Transfer to an ice cream maker and freeze according to manufacturer's instructions. Alternatively, transfer to a shallow metal tray and freeze, whisking every couple of hours until frozen and creamy. Freeze overnight.

Makes 4 cups

Dreaming of baklava? It's all here . . . a superb mixture of phyllo pastry, nuts, honey, citrus, and spice—and ice cream!

baklava ice cream

2/3 cup milk
13/4 cups light whipping cream
2 tablespoons honey
1/3 cup superfine sugar
1 teaspoon ground cinnamon
2 strips orange zest
4 egg yolks
1/3 cup pistachios, toasted
   and chopped

1/3 cup walnuts, toasted
   and chopped
6 sheets phyllo pastry
2 tablespoons unsalted butter,
   melted
confectioners' sugar,
   for dusting

Put the milk, cream, honey, sugar, cinnamon, and orange zest in a saucepan over medium heat. Stirring constantly, cook for a few minutes or until the sugar dissolves and the mixture is just about to boil. Remove from the heat.

Whisk the egg yolks in a large bowl. Whisk in 1/4 cup of the hot milk mixture until smooth. Whisk in the remainder, then return to a clean saucepan and stir constantly over low–medium heat for 8–10 minutes or until the mixture coats the back of a spoon. Do not allow to boil. Cool slightly, then cover and refrigerate until cold. Remove the orange zest.

Gently stir most of the pistachios into the custard, reserving some for decoration. Transfer to an ice cream maker and freeze according to manufacturer's instructions. Alternatively, transfer to a shallow metal tray and freeze, whisking every couple of hours until frozen and creamy.

Brush a sheet of phyllo pastry with butter, then scrunch up into a flat "rose" shape about 3$\frac{1}{4}$ inches across. Put on a cookie sheet lined with baking paper. Repeat with the remaining pastry and butter, brushing any leftover butter over the tops. Bake for 10–12 minutes or until golden. Cool.

Serve scoops of ice cream topped with phyllo rounds, sprinkled with nuts, dusted with confectioners' sugar, and drizzled with extra honey if desired.

Serves 6

baklava ice cream

black sesame seed ice cream

¹/₃ cup black sesame seeds,
   toasted
3 cups milk
1 cup light whipping cream

1 teaspoon vanilla extract
³/₄ cup superfine sugar
6 egg yolks

Grind the sesame seeds to a rough powder using a mortar and pestle or spice mill, and put in a saucepan with the milk, cream, and vanilla. Stirring constantly, cook over medium heat for several minutes or until the sugar dissolves and the milk is just about to boil. Remove from the heat.

Whisk the sugar and egg yolks in a large bowl. Whisk in ¹/₄ cup of the hot milk mixture until smooth. Whisk in the remainder, then return to a clean saucepan and stir constantly over low–medium heat for 8–10 minutes or until the mixture thickens and coats the back of a spoon. Do not allow to boil. Cool slightly, then cover and refrigerate until cold.

Transfer to an ice cream maker and freeze according to manufacturer's instructions. Alternatively, transfer to a shallow metal tray and freeze, whisking every couple of hours until frozen and creamy. Freeze for 5 hours or overnight. Soften in the fridge for 30 minutes before serving.

Makes 4 cups

honeydew and midori sorbet

large knob of fresh ginger,
  thinly sliced
1 large handful mint, roughly
  chopped
3/4 cup superfine sugar

2 pounds 4 ounces very ripe
  honeydew melon
3 egg whites
3 tablespoons Midori or other
  melon liqueur

Put the ginger and mint in a small saucepan with 1 1/2 cups water. Bring to a boil, then reduce the heat and simmer for 5 minutes. Stir in the sugar and simmer for an additional 5 minutes. Remove from the heat and cool. Blend or process until finely chopped, then strain.

Peel and seed the melon and purée until smooth—you should have about 3 cups of purée. Stir in the ginger syrup. Transfer to an ice cream maker and freeze according to manufacturer's instructions, adding the egg whites and liqueur halfway through. Alternatively, transfer to a shallow metal tray and freeze, whisking every couple of hours until frozen and smooth, adding the egg whites and liqueur during the final beating. Freeze for 4 hours or overnight. Store in the freezer until ready to serve.

Makes 4 cups

Star anise adds star quality to luscious mango in this
beautifully refreshing sorbet.

mango and star anise sorbet

heaping 3/4 cup superfine
   sugar
2 star anise
1 tablespoon lemon juice
4 large ripe mangoes,
   chopped
2 egg whites

honey macadamia wafers
1 egg white
1/4 cup superfine sugar
2 tablespoons honey
2 tablespoons all-purpose
   flour, sifted
2 tablespoons unsalted butter,
   melted and cooled
3/4 cup macadamia nuts, finely
   chopped

Put the sugar, 1 1/4 cups water, and the star anise in a saucepan. Stir over
medium heat until the sugar has dissolved. Bring to a boil, then reduce
the heat and simmer for 1 minute. Set aside to cool to room temperature.
Stir in the lemon juice.

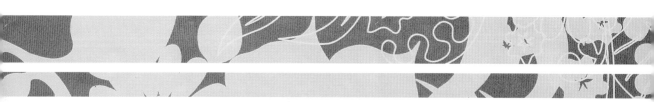

Purée the mango in a food processor until smooth. Strain the sugar syrup into the mango and process until just combined. Transfer to an ice cream machine and freeze according to manufacturer's instructions. Alternatively, transfer to a shallow metal tray and freeze, whisking every couple of hours until frozen and smooth. Freeze for 4 hours or overnight. Store in the freezer until ready to serve.

Preheat the oven to 400°F. Line two cookie sheets with baking paper. To make the honey macadamia wafers, beat the egg white in a small bowl with electric beaters until soft peaks form. Gradually add the sugar and continue beating until the sugar has dissolved. Beat in the honey, then fold in the flour and butter. Spread very thinly over the prepared trays, then sprinkle with macadamias. Bake for 7–10 minutes or until lightly golden. Set aside to cool on the trays, then break into pieces. Serve at once with scoops of mango sorbet.

Serves 6

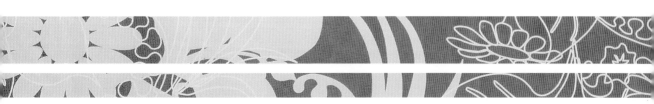

mango and star anise sorbet

honey parfait with caramelized kumquats

1/4 cup honey

4 egg yolks

1 1/4 cups light whipping cream,
  lightly whipped and chilled

1 tablespoon Grand Marnier

1 pound 2 ounces kumquats

1 1/2 cups superfine sugar

Bring the honey to a boil in a small saucepan. Beat the egg yolks in a bowl until thick and pale, then add the hot honey in a slow stream, beating until cooled. Gently fold in the cream and liqueur, combining well. Pour into six 1/2-cup molds. Freeze for 4 hours or until firm.

Prick each kumquat with a skewer and place in a large saucepan. Cover with boiling water and simmer for 20 minutes. Strain 2 cups of the liquid into a saucepan, then add the sugar and stir over medium heat until the sugar has dissolved. Increase the heat and boil for 10 minutes. Add the kumquats and simmer for 20 minutes or until the kumquats are soft, with smooth, shiny skins. Set aside to cool.

To serve, briefly dip the molds in hot water, then invert the parfaits onto serving plates. Serve with the caramelized kumquats and a little kumquat syrup spooned over the top.

Serves 6

plum wine ice

1/2 cup superfine sugar
a few lemon zest strips
2 tablespoons fresh ginger,
   thinly sliced

1 pound 2 ounces ripe plums,
   pits removed
2 cups Japanese plum wine
   (ume shu)

Put the sugar, lemon zest, ginger, and 11/2 cups water in a saucepan over medium heat. Stirring constantly, cook for a few minutes or until the sugar dissolves. Bring to a boil, then reduce the heat and simmer for 10 minutes. Cool completely, then strain.

Purée the plums in a food processor, then strain through a fine sieve, pushing down to extract the juice—you should have about 1 cup. Add to the cooled syrup with the plum wine, then pour into a shallow tray and freeze for 21/2 hours or until the mixture starts to freeze around the edges.

Scrape the frozen edges back into the mixture with a fork. Repeat every 30 minutes for 3 hours or until evenly sized ice crystals form. If preparing the granita ahead of time, store it in the freezer and scrape once again just before serving. To serve, scrape into dishes with a fork.

Makes 4 cups

Rosy-hued Turkish delight is an exquisite ice cream flavoring.

Pomegranate seeds add a hedonistic touch.

turkish delight ice cream

1¹/₂ cups milk
2 cups light whipping cream
²/₃ cup superfine sugar
6 egg yolks

3¹/₂ ounces good-quality, rose
water–flavored Turkish
delight, roughly chopped
2 tablespoons pomegranate
seeds

Put 1 cup of the milk in a saucepan with the cream and sugar. Cook over medium heat, stirring constantly for a few minutes, until the sugar has dissolved and the mixture is just about to boil. Remove from the heat.

Whisk the egg yolks in a bowl until well combined, then whisk in ¹/₄ cup of the hot milk mixture. Whisk in the remaining milk mixture until smooth, then return to a clean saucepan and stir constantly over low–medium heat for 8–10 minutes or until the mixture thickens and coats the back of a spoon. Do not allow to boil. Strain through a fine sieve and set aside.

Put the remaining milk and the Turkish delight in a small saucepan over medium heat. Stir constantly until the Turkish delight has dissolved into the milk. Stir the mixture into the custard, allow to cool slightly, then refrigerate until cold.

Transfer to an ice cream maker and freeze according to manufacturer's instructions. Alternatively, transfer to a shallow metal tray and freeze, whisking every couple of hours until frozen and creamy. Freeze for 5 hours or overnight. Soften in the fridge for 30 minutes before serving.

Serve the ice cream drizzled with the pomegranate seeds.

Makes 4 cups

turkish delight ice cream

strawberry and banana tofu ice

10 1/2 ounces silken tofu,
   chopped
1 2/3 cups strawberries, chopped
2 ripe bananas, chopped
1/4 cup superfine sugar

Blend the tofu, strawberries, bananas, and sugar in a blender or food processor until smooth.

Transfer to an ice cream maker and freeze according to manufacturer's instructions. Alternatively, transfer to a shallow metal tray and freeze, whisking every couple of hours until frozen and smooth. Freeze for 4 hours or overnight. Store in the freezer until ready to serve.

Makes 4 cups

mango and passion fruit sorbet

1 cup superfine sugar
1/3 cup passion fruit pulp
1/2 large mango, chopped

1 large peach, chopped
2 tablespoons lemon juice
1 egg white

Put the sugar in a pan with 1 cup of water and stir over low heat until the sugar has dissolved. Increase the heat, bring to a boil, and allow to boil for 1 minute. Set aside to cool, then cover and refrigerate until cold. Strain the passion fruit pulp, reserving 1 tablespoon of the seeds.

Purée the mango, peach, passion fruit juice, and lemon juice in a blender until smooth. With the motor running, add the cold sugar syrup and 2/3 cup water. Stir in the passion fruit seeds.

Transfer to an ice cream maker and freeze according to manufacturer's instructions. Alternatively, transfer to a shallow metal tray and freeze, whisking every couple of hours until frozen and smooth. Freeze for 4 hours or overnight. Store in the freezer until ready to serve.

Makes 4 cups

Now here's the perfect finish to a restrained meal—
an uninhibited interplay of intriguing Japanese flavors.

japanese parfait

1²/₃ cups strawberries

1 cup sweet adzuki bean paste (anko)

1 cup flaked corn breakfast cereal

3 tablespoons black sesame seeds, lightly toasted

6 scoops green tea ice cream (see page 356)

6 scoops Japanese red bean ice cream (see page 343)

¹/₃ cup Japanese black sugar syrup (anmitsu sauce)

2 tablespoons Japanese sweet soybean powder (kinako)

Hull and slice the strawberries. Place a tablespoon of the bean paste in each of six tall sundae glasses, then sprinkle a few strawberry slices over each.

Combine the cornflakes and sesame seeds and divide half the mixture between the glasses. Place a scoop of green tea ice cream in each glass.

Dollop another tablespoon of the bean paste over each ice cream scoop and press down lightly to smooth over.

Divide the remaining strawberry slices between the glasses and sprinkle over the remaining cornflake mixture.

Add a scoop of red bean ice cream to each glass and press down to compact slightly. Drizzle each parfait with the black sugar syrup, then drop a heaping teaspoon of the sweet soybean powder on top of each. Serve immediately with long spoons.

Serving suggestion: Make a Japanese-style sundae by putting a scoop of Japanese red bean and green tea ice cream (see pages 343 and 356) in a sundae glass and serve with extra sweet adzuki bean paste and/or a good-quality chocolate sauce—all these flavors go well together, as does adzuki bean paste, banana, and toasted walnuts.

Serves 6

index

407

409

411

413

Arrowroot powder – natural thickening for milk.

Rice Powder – or Tapioca starch Powder ✓ – Cream Cheese

ricotta cannoli semifreddo 108

rocky road ice cream 238

rose geranium sorbet 65

rosemary, carrot, and orange granita 76

ruby red grapefruit granita 133

rum

coffee, rum, and walnut ice cream 264

rum and raisin ice cream 17

saffron and raisin ice cream 385

sahlab ice cream 9, 367

sake, Nashi pear and sake sorbet 348

semifreddo

Amaretti 146

with caramel oranges 121

chocolate and hazelnut 170

cinnamon 138

espresso 181

ricotta cannoli 108

torrone 132

walnut 104

sesame seeds

black sesame seed ice cream 390

Japanese parfait 404

sesame halva ice cream 373

supernatural 218

sherbet 10

lemon and lime 47

sherry trifle ice cream 22

sorbet

apple and pear 94

apricot and orange blossom 83

bellini 152

black currant 23

blood orange 145

cantaloupe 109

cherry 114

chianti 175

chili, lime, and lemon grass 330

guava 332

kiwi fruit 379

mango and passion fruit 403

mango and star anise 392

Moroccan mint tea 336

nashi pear and sake 348

nectarine 139

papaya lime 325

peach and rosewater 366

pineapple 231

rose geranium 65

strawberry 52

vanilla-scented rhubarb sorbet 66

sour cream ice cream 48

spice

chai ice cream 374

spiced cherry brandy sundae 289

star anise, mango and star anise sorbet 392

strawberries

Japanese parfait 404

lychee and strawberry ice cream 362

strawberry and balsamic granita 157

strawberry and banana tofu ice 402

strawberry ice cream 29

strawberry shortcake ice cream 272

strawberry sorbet 52

tutti fruitti bombe 284

sundaes

big peach 270

blueberry port 252

chocolate 202

chunky monkey chocolate peanut butter 248

Hawaiian 302

hazelnut heaven ice cream 314

mocha custard 318

spiced cherry brandy 289

supernatural 218

tamarillo ice cream 384

414

415